Mike Epstein on Hitting

COACHES
CHOICE™

ISBN: 1-58518-777-1
Library of Congress Control Number: 2002116612
Cover design: Kerry Hartjen
Text design: Jeanne Hamilton
Front cover photo: Ken Jacques
Text photos: Ken Jacques — pages 11, 30, 39, 43, 49, 55, 63, 126, 132, 163

Coaches Choice
P.O. Box 1828
Monterey, CA 93942
www.coacheschoice.com

DEDICATION

I am especially indebted to my mentor, Ted Williams, for his never-ending passion, questions and genius. It was at Ted's insistence that I become "more visible." He urged me to position myself to be more influential in furnishing and simplifying proper hitting technique for today's players. How could I refuse? Very few have been afforded the extraordinary opportunity to interact and share intellectual ideas with the "world's greatest hitter." I am indeed humble—and fortunate—and will never forget.

And to my soul mate, lifetime companion and wife, Barbara, for inspiring me to undertake these worthwhile projects.

And to my son, Jake, a terrific baseball player in his own right, who has given me innumerable reasons to continue learning and to share the wealth of information I have accumulated down through the years.

ACKNOWLEDGMENTS

Ted Williams used to lament that he could go into a bookstore and find fifty books on how to hit a golf ball, but couldn't find one on how to hit a baseball that was worth reading. Hopefully, this book will address that concern.

Accordingly, at this point, I would like to acknowledge the many baseball people who helped make this compendium a reality by sharing their experiences and hitting philosophies with me over the years. And equally important, to those who were kind enough to play "devil's advocate"—and disagreed with me—enabling me to defuse the complexity of simply hitting a baseball. Without their dissent and friendship, it would have been impossible to dissociate "style" from "technique"—and "fact from fiction."

I sincerely hope you enjoy this compendium of hitting articles and that you are able to use this valuable information to reach your coaching or hitting potential.

Mike Epstein

FOREWORD

For the past ten years, I have run a very successful baseball school. When baseball is your profession, it becomes very important to seek out the highest quality information. As such, I have attended hundreds of lectures, clinics, and conventions and have heard lots of interesting speakers. Many of these efforts involved coaches, who either repeated a common hitting philosophy—combined their own "spin," or former players, who tried to teach you to hit "like they did." Most made some interesting points, told great stories, and provided some useful drills, but none were able to objectively say how the "best" players in baseball hit.

Over the years, I have attempted to develop my own theories concerning hitting. The result was a hodge podge of good thinking and ideas from other coaches and players. In 2002, my hitting education went to a whole new level. I decided to give Mike Epstein a call. Mike and I both write for *Collegiate Baseball News*, and I had read some of his articles. I don't even remember why I called. But, I am sure glad I did.

For the next two hours, Mike turned my hitting world upside down. Mike has been able to take all of the "conventional" wisdom out of hitting instruction and to create a method of instruction that can be utilized by major leaguers and also understood by the everyday little league coach. As soon as I got off the phone, I wanted to go and teach what I had learned. Mike's philosophy on hitting, as you will see in this book, is more than just informative—it is exciting! I found myself thinking about our conversation for the next few weeks and applying many of his teaching techniques.

The results were amazing. My students were hitting like they never have before and saying things like, "I feel like I'm doing so little but hitting the ball so hard" and "it feels like I have so much more time."

This book is a collection of Mike Epstein's articles from publications like *Collegiate Baseball News*. The articles, presented in no particular order, are meant to be stand-alone essays on the various subjects of hitting. Most were derived from the most common questions Mike has received on the Forum on his web site (www.MikeEpsteinHitting.com).

I hope this book is as much fun for you to read as it was for me to help compile.

Paul Reddick
Owner, New Jersey Baseball Academy

CONTENTS

INTRODUCTION

As many of you know, I played for Ted Williams for three years when he managed the Washington Senators, and later mentored under him for many years after I retired from baseball. Ted gave me his only known written letter of recommendation on hitting instruction; I am deeply honored to have earned it. I cherish the last multi-hour visit we had in his suite at the U.S. Grant Hotel in San Diego a few years back, discussing hitting in particular, and life in general.

Spending many, many days and nights at his home in Florida over the years, has been a true highlight of my life, and has given me a rare personal perspective on this great man. A clip of Ted on my hitting video simply says, "I consider Mike one of my very best friends." I considered Ted one of my very best friends, also.

I can vividly remember Louise Kauffman, who lived with Ted for many years, saying one day, "Mike, you know you and Bobby Doerr (Red Sox Hall-of-Fame second baseman) are the only two friends Ted has ever allowed into our bedroom."

Ted loved to intimidate people, and, at first, I proved no exception. He'd insult me, berate me, and tell me he was "wasting his time" mentoring me. He'd cuss at me, laugh at my ideas, and continually chide me by saying "for a smart guy, you sure ask dumb questions!" But, once you got to know Ted, you know this was his *modus operandi*. Scant moments later, he would bellow "That's right! Boy oh boy! You're on to something there! Keep going with it. Go on! NOW, what if a hitter could ..." or "Do you think that ...." And we'd be off on yet another tangent. You get the picture.

He was tough. *Very tough*. He reminded me of Sean Connery in Finding Forrester, a movie I thoroughly enjoyed because of the mentor-student relationship. Like Connery, Ted had his own inimitable way of challenging me to help take our conversations to the next level. Many times he would put me on the brink of total frustration and intimidation and then suddenly stop short-and-almost whispering—say something like, "Do you realize the things we're talking about here? *Nobody* talks about these things." The gentleness of his tone made me realize the respect he had for me and the sanctity of our level of discussion. It was then that I realized both the agony and the ecstasy of interacting with—and being mentored by—this thoroughly brilliant, unique, and dynamic man.

I have said countless times, being mentored by Ted Williams has given me insights into hitting afforded to very few. I take absolutely no credit for these insights; only the ability to crystallize them in a way hitters can understand and use effectively to hit their potentials.

Thanks, skipper, for sharing your perceptions, knowledge and experiences with me. And for keeping me challenged and focused throughout the years in the pursuit of simplifying the toughest thing to do in all of sports. I only hope I am up to the task in your absence.

Needless to say, his passing is a tremendous loss for not only me and my family, but also for the rest of my fellow Americans.

Ted used to say that "a good hitter hitting in the strike zone is three times more effective than a great hitter hitting outside the strike zone." To this I would simply add, rest in peace, my dear friend, and "get a good pitch to hit."

Mike and Ted Williams
U.S. Grand Hotel, San Diego, Ca 2000

PART I

The Movements of 95% of Baseball's Hall of Fame Hitters

CHAPTER 1

Keep It "Simple" For Success

My telephone wouldn't stop ringing after last summer's all-star game. Concerned parents saying, "I didn't see one player on this year's all-star team batting like my son is being taught. And confused players saying, "I didn't see anyone 'squishing the bug,' or 'watching the ball hit the bat,' or 'swinging down at the ball,' or 'hitting on their front foot,' like my coach tells me to do. What gives?"

What exactly is it about mechanics that confuses us so that we can't even "see" the mechanics of the players that grab all the headlines and make all the money? When parents and players are asking questions like the ones above, we coaches have a problem. WE should be telling THEM about the changes going on. We should be on the cusp, teaching leading-edge mechanics. But this isn't happening. Is it because we don't know what to look for? Is it because we teach what we hear? Or read? Or teach what we were taught when we were playing? Is it because today's proliferation of instant information—both good and bad—that's made hitting so confusing?

Emulation

It seems EVERYONE has their own idea of the perfect swing and the mechanics that go along with it. I think there may not be an activity as intensely discussed, debated, and opinionated as teaching hitting.

Over the years, I have garnered a good reputation for being able to simplify the swing process and present it in a very understandable way. In reality, there were no hitting coaches when I broke into professional baseball, back in 1965. Baseball was a whole lot simpler back then. The hitting technique used was passed on from generation to generation, beginning with "Shoeless" Joe Jackson at the turn of the twentieth century. Babe Ruth copied him, and baseball was "off to the races." The more success Ruth enjoyed, the more he was "copied" by other players. It's just the nature of the game. If HE'S getting it done, maybe he's doing it "right." Make no mistake about it: emulation has played a very significant part of the learning process. And still does.

Knowing I played for Ted Williams on the Washington Senators and mentored under him, people ask why I would teach the mechanics he used. Their reasoning is Ted had "special" talents, the ONLY person who could hit that way. Actually, nothing could be further from the truth! As Babe copied Shoeless Joe, and everyone attempted to copy Ruth, so did Williams copy those before him. Ted's mechanics mirrored the mechanics of other successful hitters in his day—and before him. Emulation is a fabulous teacher. Make no mistake about it, it has taught mechanics to more players than any other learning/teaching method. Unfortunately, it is an exceedingly slow and tedious process, often taking years to complete. And, not everyone has the ability for their own internal "camera" to go "click-click"—take the correct "picture"—and effectively use the information.

Many players never get it right until after they get to the big leagues. Slowly but surely, these players change through emulation. If they don't adjust, they don't stay. Pretty simple. The process is so slow it often goes unnoticed. That's why some players "come into their own" later in their careers. The "bell" suddenly goes off. How many times do we hear baseball people say about a 22-year old who has size, but shows little power: "He'll be fine. He'll get stronger as he gets older." Believe me, he won't be any stronger at 32 than at 22. If he starts to hit for power, it's because he made the "right" adjustments, getting his body into more advantaged hitting positions. He learns this by watching other players do it, time after time.

"Simple" is the Key

Ted Williams repeatedly told me that a good hitting instructor has got to make it simple. What you, as an instructor, have to know to teach, your students don't have to know to learn. Don't use scientific terms—just good common, everyday analogies and examples from your baseball career to which players can relate. All the product knowledge in the world is worth little, unless the player can internalize and use the good information you articulate to him. "Keep it simple," he would say over and over, "and understandable." Over the past twenty years, I have followed his advice religiously. It has served me and all my students well.

Part of the problem are the "cues" we use, because in reality, they are baffling and often less than correct. Phrases like "turn and burn," "grip it and rip it," and even "see the ball, hit the ball" do little to help a hitter. And, how about "watch the ball hit the bat," "squish the bug," "throw your hands at the ball," "swing down for backspin," and "keep the barrel of the bat above the hands." These don't teach mechanics. If we use these, we must tell the player that they are nothing more than "coaching truisms," and not "mechanical truisms." But, we rarely—if ever—do, and players hang on to every word we tell them. I asked Williams a number of years ago if he ever saw the ball hit the bat. He said no. Neither did I.

The other day a player started lessons with me, and I asked him why he felt the need for private instruction. He said he was making contact, but had no power and hit too many ground balls. I asked him what he was being taught to do, and he responded, "to swing down and stay back." I asked him to take a few "dry" swings for me, emphasizing "swinging down and staying back" at the same time. He took a few swings, looked up, and said, "Mike, you can't do both at the same time!" No wonder hitters today are confused. Often, we teach hitting movements that defy biomechanics and physics, tugging hitters in totally opposite directions. We need to simplify to help these players hit their potential and help get them to the next level.

In my experience, there are very few stones that have been left unturned when it comes to hitting. The information is out there. We just have to be smart enough to sort out the enormous amount of information, simplify it, and present it.

Style and Technique

To get an initial handle on this issue, we must define the words "style" and "technique." Unfortunately, these words have been used interchangeably over the years. We hear people talking about players having their own "hitting styles." I think this is confusing. What does it really mean? In reality, there are only two hitting techniques: upper body (linear) and lower body (rotational). Players are one or the other. While it may be possible to combine both hitting systems, my experience is that such an approach is restraining for even the elite athlete. Over the years, linear hitting has produced singles and contact hitters, while rotational hitters have been the power hitters and run producers.

❑ *Style*. Style IS the player. Style is what distinguishes him from everyone else. Style is personal. A number of years ago at an Oakland A's Old Timers' game, Vida Blue, Catfish Hunter, Reggie Jackson, and I were standing against the left centerfield fence. We were laughing and telling "war stories" when a player on the opposing team stepped into the batting cage to hit. "Who's that?" asked Vida. None of us recognized the player. Then, as he knocked some dirt out of his spikes, in unison, we said, "Danny Cater!" Although we couldn't see his face, his mannerisms (style) told us all we needed to know. We all have our own personal styles, and they allow us to do things as effortlessly and comfortably as possible. You've done the same thing, recognizing people by the way they walk when you weren't close enough to really "see" them.

When we bat, we utilize our personal style to get our bodies into advantaged hitting positions. All the pre-swing movements we make, we should do as relaxing as possible. Some of us are "quiet" hitters, some have wide stances, some have deep crouches, and some have their hands high. When an instructor says you have to be "comfortable," he's talking about your style. In other words, the goal is to be "tension-free."

❑ *Technique*. On the other hand, we have "technique." Technique is not personal. Technique is universal. 95% of baseball's Hall of Fame used the same technique. The core movements of this technique are 1) the hips lead the hands, 2) matching the plane of the swing to the plane of the pitch, and 3) staying inside the ball. There is a fourth, starting on time, but, in my opinion, this is not technique. Over the past century, baseball's productive (high OPS) players have hit this way. Ultimately, the player's personal style will "wrap around" the universal technique. It is why hitters all "look" different, but utilize the same core movements from launch to contact to follow-through. They all have different styles, but the technique remains constant. What's made it so difficult to see is it happens in milliseconds and often goes unnoticed.

Art or Science?

Much has been written about whether hitting is an "art" or a "science." But, which is it? Art or science? Is it really "either/or?" Many individuals will argue for one or the other, but I believe hitting encompasses BOTH words. I hope I've made my point that the "art" of the swing is the "style," and the "science" is the "technique."

Now that we have laid down the basics to simplify the swing by separating "style" from "technique," we can zero in on the core mechanical movements of baseball's elite hitters. In this compendium, we'll explore these three core movements used by 95% of baseball's Hall of Fame hitters. First, we'll tackle core movement #1, "the hips lead the hands." Over the past one hundred years, this biomechanical movement has proven to be the root of all speed and power in the swing. We'll look at how, why, and where in the swing it happens, and the profound effect it makes on bat quickness, bat velocity, and power.

CHAPTER 2

The Hips Lead the Hands

When simplifying the complexities of the productive swing, the previous chapter discussed the major impacts that *emulation, style,* and *technique* played in the learning process. This article reviews the *core mechanical movements of the productive swing,* beginning with the concepts of torque and the *"hips leading the hands."* The following chapters deal with the core mechanical movements of "matching the plane of the swing to the plane of the pitch" and "staying inside the ball".

Hitters Can Learn It from the Pitchers

Many times we hear coaches talking about the similarities between pitching and hitting. And there are many. When I was playing, coaches used to tell me that, also, but never explain what the "similarities" were.

In the photo, *Greg Maddux* is seen in the "torque position." Often we hear "torque" being generated in pitching and hitting, but I believe very few understand its proper definition. Put simply and understandably, torque is nothing more than two forces working simultaneously in opposite directions on an object. (While there are various "torquing" movements within the swing itself, we'll concentrate on this particular, dominant torquing action.) In the photo, we see one force going forward (lower body) and one force going rearward (upper body), with BOTH forces working on the player's "axis" (the imaginary "pole" extending perpendicularly from the button on the player's cap down through his body. Here, you see Maddux's lower body opening up (rotating forward) as his front foot plants, while his upper body is going back (rotating rearward).Torque in action! This is a scientifically proven, biomechanically correct movement in the "kinetic chain," called the "kinetic link." It is the root of all speed and power in physical movement. When a pitcher gets into this position, he has the

Photo credit: Stephen Dunn/Allsport

momentum of the biggest and strongest muscles in his body (the legs) pulling the smaller and weaker ones (hands/arms) through. Voila! The perfect pitching position AND the perfect hitting position.

This separation between the upper and lower halves is a relatively easy movement to teach in pitching. All (nearly all) pitchers get into this position. Not so with all hitters. While baseball's ELITE (productive) major league hitters get themselves to this very SAME position, teaching it has been extremely difficult. Yet, 95% of baseball's Hall of Fame hitters have done it correctly. How did they learn it, if few teach it? Once again. emulation in action! The photo of *Barry Bonds* shows him "winding the rubber band" in the classic torque position: hips "open," top half "closed." (FYI, I call the counter-rotational move, "winding the rubber band." Players really take to it—they understand the concept.)

If you also think of hitting as a "fly-rod" effect, I think players can get the picture a bit easier: when the fly runs out of line and gets yanked forward in the cast, it is akin to the front heel planting and yanking the hands forward. This factor is clearly shown in my videotape, "Do We Teach What We Really See?"

OK, Mike You've Convinced Me. How Does It "Happen?"

To put it simply, "the hips leading the hands" is a dynamic moment in the swing. In the "take away," or pre-swing, as the upper body starts rearward, the front shoulder comes down and in somewhat, the weight "shifting," becoming balanced or sometimes *slightly forward*, to the inside of the front thigh. What is important here is the hands,

arms, and upper body go back together, keeping the elbows "soft," not rigid. By that I mean, the hands, arms, and upper body turn back TOGETHER—as a "unit," not separately. This will maintain the integrity of the soft elbows. The hands should be somewhere near the rear shoulder, roughly 3"-8" in towards the plate. The goal is a "tension-free" swing—nothing at this point should be tensed up.

Now, as the player is "counter-rotating" on top, his lower half is beginning to open in the stride. This happens a fraction later than the top-side counter-rotation. The stride foot should be at a minimum 45-degree angle, open enough to allow the hips to come through. (I recommend and teach a very short stride.) He should land on his TOES, because when the player drops his heel, the swing is then triggered. The swing doesn't take place until AFTER the front heel plants! When it does plant, the player is then in the proper torque position (top half going back, lower half coming forward). This whole movement takes place in milliseconds. Remember, at this point—the heel dropping—the legs burst forward, initiating their rotational path. BUT, THE HANDS ARE STILL GOING BACKWARD! (Remember the definition of "torque?" – two forces acting in opposite direction on an object.) The forward momentum of the big muscles (legs) then yank the small muscles (hands and arms) forward, maximizing bat quickness, bat velocity, and power.

When it is time to swing—when the front heel drops—the hands will be automatically "yanked" to the ball by the explosive forward movement of the rotating hips. (To counteract the straightening of the lead elbow at this point, some "tension" may be used on the lead arm. The violent yanking of the hands can involuntarily straighten out the lead arm by leaving the hands back.) So, keep an eye out for the player who separates his hands from his body, straightening his lead arm. If a player does this (pre-extends the lead arm), his initial move to the ball will be away from his body (thereby making him pre-disposed to hitting around the ball). Also, watch for the player who wants to "cock" his bottom wrist at the launch position, an action which puts the barrel of the bat over (and sometimes past) his head, potentially creating a longer swing and "timing" problems. You may, in fact, see some successful big leaguers doing this. But, in my opinion, for every successful one, there have probably been jillions who made premature exits from the game. It's very difficult to master correctly.

The object is to get the longest (most) separation of the upper and lower halves and then, at launch, the shortest time lapse before the hands get yanked forward by the rotating hips. It is for this reason why we are often baffled by players who are not very big, but generate tremendous power.

But, what about the big player who has little power? ("Powerless effort versus effortless power.") I see this all too often. Mostly, the players don't get their bodies positioned correctly and don't get their legs working correctly in the swing. It all starts with the feet and works upward (kinetic chain). I read a report that up until a few years ago, 42 of the top 50 home run hitters in ML history weighed less than 190 lbs! Contrary to popular belief, power CAN be taught. It all starts with proper mechanics.

But, this isn't solely about power hitting. It's about *production*. High on-base percentage plus high slugging percentage (OPS). Ask any ML manager if they would rather have their club lead the league in batting average and in the middle of the pack in runs, or lead the league in runs scored with a team BA of .250. What do you think they tell me? You're right. RUNS WIN BALL GAMES.

Balance. Balance. Balance

But, also remember, that to teach or learn this effectively, the player must regain the balance point in the stride, because without proper preparation (balance), the dynamic sequencing of the torque goes for naught; it is virtually impossible to rotate the hips optimally using only "one" leg. Proper rotation requires both legs balanced to ensure maximum rotational velocity. Many times you will see a major league hitter holding weight on his back side (loading up) in his stance, but when he strides, he re-gains the balance point. If the player doesn't (transfer his weight correctly), two things happen: 1) he will collapse his back side, creating a swing gradient much too steep for the plane of the pitch, or 2) he will displace an equal amount of weight forward, in the approach phase, onto his front side, causing his body to lunge. In my proprietary drills, to help ensure this from happening, I advocate getting a little bit more weight forward in the stride, because when the front heel drops, the rear shoulder begins to dip. And as the rear shoulder dips, it "allows" the lead elbow to start working slightly upward. As this happens, the player's weight AUTOMATICALLY shifts back to the inside of the rear thigh; his forward movement is "blocked," and the momentum revolves (rotates) around the axis. Try it! When people ask me how to stop a player from lunging, this is what I show them. It works!

Torque Angle

There IS a way to measure the amount of torque in the swing. I call this the "torque angle." To measure torque angle, we must use an overhead view of the hitter. This angle is measured WHEN THE FRONT FOOT PLANTS. It is accomplished by drawing lines through the open hips and closed shoulders of the player. The angle generated by the intersecting lines is the torque angle (See Figure 2-1).

One thing to remember when teaching this factor is that "thinner" players can stretch their midsections more than "thicker" players. Fact of life. It's why Ken Griffey, Jr's torque "angle" is 40° (the most in major league baseball), and Mark McGwire's was little more than half that. BUT, the thicker player many times makes up for the lesser torque angle with greater strength. Things seem to balance out in the long run. But the productive ones all get to the torque position! The point here is a player can only go so far counter-rotating on top, as his lower half opens—his body structure will limit it. So, when working with a player, make sure he doesn't go back too far on top and lose his ability to see the pitch with both eyes! The pre-swing (the stride and counter-rotation) is for "rhythm," timing, and "winding the rubber band," without which we would really struggle as hitters.

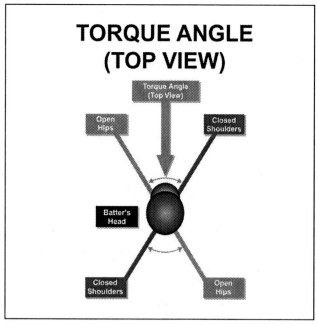

Figure 2-1. Torque angle (top view)

Tiger Woods is a topical sports figure and a terrific example of torque. I read where his torque angle has been measured at 80°, which is why he is able to out-drive his competition weighing 60-70 pounds more. "Effortless power versus powerless effort." If you are wondering why Woods' torque angle is twice that of Griffey, Jr's, it's because golfers don't have to get back to contact at any given point in time. They can keep going back on their takeaways until THEY are ready to address the ball. Baseball players don't have this luxury! Our hands are yanked forward before they can get them back too far, limiting the angle. Our timing must be perfect.

At What Point Do We Get into the "Torque Position?"

As discussed earlier, dropping the heel with the front foot initiates the hips, putting the hitter into the torque position. WHEN this actually occurs is entirely dependent on each individual hitter, his personal "resources," the "plan" he took to the plate, his anticipation of certain pitches with less than two strikes, and his mechanics. So, all I can do is give you an approximation. Obviously, the longer one can wait, the better.

I have a video sequence of Babe Ruth in the 1920s, taken from the top of the grandstands in St. Louis. His heel dropped when the pitch was about 10' in front of the plate, and he pulled a line drive to right field. However, I couldn't tell you the velocity of the pitch. It may have been an off-speed pitch. Good mechanics, however, will give the hitter more time to make his decision whether to swing—or not swing. And, many times, this fractional second in time separates the "prospects" from the "suspects." Time ultimately becomes the hitter's greatest ally—or enemy. My mentor, Ted Williams, always told me to "wait—and be quick!"

Generally speaking, though, if the pitch is perceived as a good pitch to hit, the front heel will drop when the pitch is approximately 15' from the plate. However, the batter can still drop the heel and hold off his swing at the last moment if the pitch works its way out of the strike zone. Good rotational mechanics allow us this benefit, because we're "not coming forward" and getting our weight to our front side. Once that weight comes forward, it's pretty tough to stop.

The Importance of Good Mechanics

After all these years of teaching, I have become partial to certain idiosyncrasies and tenets of the swing. I seem to base what I teach on not as much "theory" as "what seems to work"—can I teach it? My job is to get hitters to hit their potential—to get them to the next level. Good mechanics play a large role in this developmental process. Yet, many times, we underestimate the impact mechanics have on our performance.

In the recent Olympics, Marion Jones, America's top female sprinter, put on an eyebrow-raising exhibition, unquestionably establishing herself as the world's fastest woman. I also read a report that she can stand under a basketball hoop and hit her elbows on the rim! Quite a physical "package." A world-class jumper and sprinter; two prime requisites for a gold medal in the long jump event. Yet, she wound up taking a bronze medal in that event, finishing *third*. When queried by a reporter whether she was disappointed in not winning a gold medal, she replied that she wasn't and actually considered herself fortunate to even win the bronze medal. She went on to say that no one had taught her the mechanics for this event; she had no technique.

How many "gold-medal athletes" are there playing baseball—right now—who will wind up with "bronze-medal careers" because they don't have the mechanics that can take them to the next level?

CHAPTER 3

Matching the Plane of the Swing to the Plane of the Pitch

The previous chapter examined the major impact that the first core mechanical movement, torque, and "winding the rubber band," have on bat quickness, bat speed, and power. This article discusses the second core mechanical movement of the productive swing, "matching the plane of the swing to the plane of the pitch."

What is the "Natural" Swing?

When I speak of the swing, I am speaking of the "natural" swing. The natural swing starts in the vicinity of the rear shoulder, initially follows a downward path, levels off approximately four inches in front of the lead knee, and then begins its upslope to finish in the vicinity of the front shoulder. Essentially, it's DOWN—LEVEL—UP. In theory, then, more lower trajectory hits should be to the opposite field; more higher trajectory hits will be pulled. Why is this? Because to hit the pitch middle-half away, the batter MUST let the ball get "deep." This puts his contact zone in the downward trajectory of the swing, theoretically producing more line drives and ground balls. Conversely, pitches middle-half in, will be hit in front of the lead knee, on the slight upslope, producing line drives and fly balls. Later in this chapter, I'll explore the effect that "timing" can have on the trajectory of the batted ball.

What is the "Level" Swing?

My definition of the "level" swing differs somewhat from what has been currently taught. When I speak of a level swing, it means LEVEL TO THE BALL—not level to the ground. And, from what I am hearing, there is a groundswell effect in the hitting community going on, which is changing its conventional thinking about the swing plane—and also its definition of the natural swing. For the past 25 years, the majority of hitters have been taught to swing "level" or "down," and to carry the initial downward plane of their swing four inches or more PAST the lead knee. This information was passed on without due regard for the fact that every pitch passing through the hitter's contact zone is going DOWN. Fast balls, sinkers, curves, sliders, change ups, and split-finger pitches all "sink" and go down. An 80-mph fastball drops 11°. At 90 mph, it drops 5-6°. At 100 mph, it drops 2-3°. Gravity and the "downward plane" see to it that all pitches go down.

All pitchers, at some point, are taught to throw in this "downward plane." Many are tall, throw off a 10-12" mound, release the ball at ear level, and aim for a point at the hitter's knees. If they can get the hitter to hit the ball on the ground, they've done their jobs well. No three-run home runs on those puppies! Make no mistake; ground balls are a pitcher's best friend. I recently read where 80% of the balls hit on the ground in the major leagues are outs. Why, then, do we teach hitters to hit GROUND BALLS? If pitchers are "taught" to THROW ground balls, why do we accommodate them? I was listening to a coach last week who was talking to his pitchers about the merits of THROWING ground balls. Twenty minutes later, he walked over to his position players and worked with them on HITTING ground balls. I really don't think some coaches think it through.

However, this thinking is finally changing. We're starting to ask ourselves, does this make sense? Is this logical? Do we really want hitters to be swinging "down" at pitches going "down?" When we "match the plane of the swing to the plane of the pitch," we're able to counteract and thwart the goal of the pitchers. Whatever pitchers do, the hitters have to adjust and do the opposite. This is what smart hitting is all about, and is a principal reason why baseball's elite manage to get there—and also why so many others never realize their lifelong dream.

The Perfect Swing is the Adjustment You Make to the Pitch You Get

In the hitter's approach phase, the *posture* of his body determines the "rough" swing plane his swing will take. Earlier, I talked about how the hitter sets his weight on the inside of his back thigh. If you'll recall, in the approach, as the batter's rear shoulder begins to dip somewhat, his rear elbow beings to tuck in close to his body. This movement allows his lead elbow to begin working up—re-setting his weight from the balanced position he established in his stride—to his weight shifting back to the inside of his rear thigh. If the batter doesn't properly go through these movements, his shoulders will remain level, his swing will be "level" to down, and his weight will go to the inside of his FRONT thigh. If you've ever tried to swing "down" and "stay back," you know exactly where I'm coming from. Yet, these are today's hitting "buzzwords."

The degree to which the player "tilts" back on his axis helps determine the gradient of his swing. For a pure power hitter, such as Mark McGwire, he will sit back further off the axis than perhaps, a line-drive gap hitter. He's got power and little foot speed, so he's looking for FLY balls. Remember, we've got to hit according to our "type." Players with less power and better foot speed will be more upright on their axis and will utilize a somewhat "flatter" swing gradient. However, the goal for the vast majority (70%) of hitters should always be line drives. Trust me, if the player has some power, he'll get his share of round trippers.

Larry Walker swinging at a high pitch. Notice his level shoulders enabling him to get on the plane of the pitch.

Barry Bonds swinging at a low pitch. Notice how he sits back on his axis, his back shoulder dipping to match the pitch plane.

As a rule, on pitches that are "up" in the strike zone, e.g., at the letters, the degree of body "tilt" lessens as the player's shoulders begin to level, and he raises his hands to get on top of the pitch (Larry Walker). By instinctively doing this, he "levels off" his swing. Pitches that are "down" at the knees will necessitate a more pronounced shoulder dip to enable the hitter to come up through the sinking ball (Barry Bonds). This is why I don't recommend—or teach—a low follow-through. Or a high one, either. The player's follow-through should naturally depend on contact location. If he swings at a low pitch, his follow-through will be somewhat higher than if he had swung at a high pitch. Proper body positioning and good mechanics go a long way toward helping the hitter achieve this core mechanical movement.

No matter which style hitter we're talking about—singles, line drive, or home run, the hips must lead the hands, to maximize bat quickness, bat speed, and power. So, while the hitter's initial posture in the approach starts him getting to the proper pitch plane, his lead elbow then becomes his "radar" detector. If you watch the lead elbows on productive hitters, you will see their lead elbows working in an approximate four inch slot. If the pitch is perceived as "down," the lead elbow works "up" in the slot. If the pitch is perceived as "up," the lead elbow makes the adjustment and works "down." I call this weathervaning™, which allows for this dynamic adjustment and "fine-tuning" of the plane of the swing to match the plane of the pitch. You see, I believe good hitting mechanics allow the hitter to make these instinctive, rapid-fire, on-the-fly adjustments to an incoming pitch. It is why I believe "the perfect swing is the adjustment you make to the pitch you get."

When players are taught to swing "one way," for example—"down," it diminishes their ability to work on the varying pitch planes. If a pitch is perceived as "down," and the player's swing has been "grooved" to swing down, the only thing he will do is hit the ball in the ground. Muscle memory always prevails. Again, why are pitchers taught to throw in a "downhill plane?" Simple. It's much tougher for the hitter to lift the ball and do some real damage unless he is able to adjust his swing. It's why my mentor, Ted Williams, said, "history is made on the inside half of the plate." Because to hit the ball on the inside-half of the plate, the batter must hit the pitch OUT IN FRONT of the lead knee—where the slight upslope of the swing occurs (Barry Bonds). Even if the pitch is down, the lead elbow—if taught correctly—will make the adjustment and work up, putting the bat in perfect alignment with the ball.

Photo credit: Al Bello/Getty Images

Maximize Your Contact Area!

Another compelling reason for "matching the plane of the swing to the plane of the pitch" is to maximize the player's contact area. If a player doesn't do this because his body movement is linear, producing an extended downward plane to his swing, he has only ONE chance to hit the ball as the planes of the swing and pitch converge. This small area of a few inches leaves little room for timing error. Contrast this to the previous example of weathervaning that produces a contact area of approximately 30" or more! For me, it's a no-brainer, yet I work with struggling players on a daily basis who have been taught to swing "down through the ball" and to hit the "top half" of the ball. This is restraining for even the elite athlete!

Get More "Punch" Out of Your Hits

Take the time, right now, and answer this question: are you EARLY—or LATE when you pop the ball up? Take your time and think. Remember, when potential is the goal, good information is vital! OK, got your answer? Ted Williams used to ask this question to hitters he met. Evidently, little thought was ever given to this question, because very few answered it correctly. This bothered Ted, because he wondered how a player could make the "proper" adjustments if he didn't know if he was early or late on a pitch.

Still have your answer in memory? OK, then follow me through. If a hitter matches the plane of his swing to the plane of the pitch—and he's a little late—he'll hit the bottom-half of the ball, producing BACKSPIN (refer to Figure 3-1). It is common knowledge that fly balls carry considerably further with backspin and should be our goal.

Now, on the other hand, if he's a little early, he'll hit the top half of the ball, producing overspin, exactly what you want on balls hit on the ground (refer to Figure 3-2). Ground balls with overspin pick up momentum as they travel, producing "bad hops" and getting by infielders too quickly for them to make a play on. You can readily see this happen when you watch a game on television with the camera behind the pitcher. When the batter's late, you'll see him swing under the ball. When he's early, he'll swing over it. Be sure to watch for it!

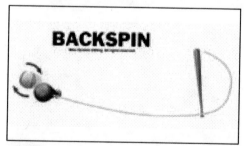

Figure 3-1

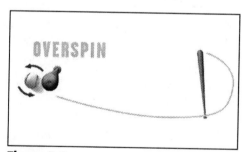

Figure 3-2

But what about pitches you time perfectly—neither early, nor late? Well, when you match the plane of the swing to the plane of the pitch, and you time it perfectly—if you're strong enough, you'll absolutely STOP the rotation on the ball. This is a frequent occurrence in professional baseball. Hitters who have batted against 60-mph knuckleballs will tell you how difficult they are to hit. Well, try catching a 100-mph knuckleball off someone's bat! Nellie Fox, the "second baseman of the decade" in the 1950s and a coach with the Washington Senators, told me he once jumped as high as he could to catch a line drive "knuckler" off a big, left-handed power hitter. The ball wound up hitting him in the left thigh. Ouch! So, either way, backspin, overspin, or knuckle ball, the hitter gets the best of all worlds when he "matches the plane of the swing to the plane of the pitch."

Over this same 25-year period, backspin was another of baseball's "buzz" words. Many players were taught to swing down to get backspin on ALL batted balls. But, when you think about it, what hitter would want backspin on ground balls? Players need to ask us logical questions, and we need to have answers for them that make sense. Why don't hitters ask these questions? If it isn't commonsensical and logical, it'll probably do the player more harm than good! We are smarter today than yesterday, and we'll be smarter tomorrow than we are today. Good information makes this possible. We've got to keep up with the times. *When potential is the goal, we must have access to good information.*

By the way, were you right or wrong? Either way, hopefully, you're a lot smarter now than before, and that this information can help you—or your players—reap huge dividends down the road.

At What Age Can the Natural Swing Be Taught?

A delicate question, indeed, because all players are different. Some mature earlier than others. Most younger players (under 12) generally lack the motor coordination needed to learn this. However, as in all cases, there are exceptions. I have had younger players progress rather nicely. Eric Chavez, the young (22 years old) and productive (26 home runs last year) Oakland A's third baseman, played on three world championship amateur teams for me. When he was 12, he had the reflexes and eye-hand coordination of someone much older. I recently worked with two eleven year olds, and both did exceptionally well. On my web site, I put a short "Before & After" video of the swing of one of them. You can find it at www.MikeEpsteinHitting.com.

Photo credit: Harry How/Getty Images

Eric Chavez, Oakland A's

Then again, given good mechanics at an early age, players will naturally "tweak" and adjust as they gain greater control of their motor coordination. By the time they reach high school, many of these players are well on their way toward being able to make the instinctive, on-the-fly adjustments I've been talking about.

More mature hitters are better able to make these mechanical adjustments through good mechanics. However, the player's inherent ability will dictate his consistency. My feeling is most players in the ML do this; the true superstars just do it more consistently.

My videotape, "Do We Teach What We Really See?" visually takes you through this instruction process, step-by-step, to learn this core movement. You'll see that to teach this, we must remember that while the back shoulder dips for a number of reasons, its singular importance is to facilitate the bat head to get on the same "rough" plane as the pitch. As the player swings, watch for the back shoulder correctly dipping and the rear elbow tucking in. As it does, it "allows" the lead elbow to work up. The player's head may also shade back an inch or two. The hitter should be directly over the rear knee, thigh perpendicular to the ground.

Alex Rodriguez

Photo credit: Brian Bahr/Allsport

This factor can be taught with a batting tee. The key point to keep in mind is that the hitter has to "learn" to hit in these areas. By making him swing at pitches "down," he will—through repetition and muscle memory—learn to dip his shoulder, and lead up with his front elbow, and hit line drives. And, by making him swing at pitches "up," he will—through repetition and muscle memory—learn to get his hands on top, thereby leveling out his swing on the high pitch, and hit line drives.

As shown in my video, these should be done initially with my Torque Drill™. As proficiency builds, graduate to my Numbers Drill™. By the time the hitter has demonstrated proficiency with both, his "game" swing should mirror what he was doing in the drills. By "teaching" the body to understand the positions it has to be in to hit these pitches, when the time comes to react, the body will already know what to do! Nothing magical here; muscle memory is the key. By the way, my experience is it takes players approximately 1,500 reps to "de-learn" and "re-learn." Patience is key.

The next chapter reviews the third core movement: "staying inside the ball"—why 10% of the players make 90% of the money.

CHAPTER 4

Staying Inside the Ball

The previous chapter detailed the major impact the second core mechanical movement, "matching the plane of the swing to the plane of the pitch," has on the baseball swing. This article, discusses the third core mechanical movement: "staying inside the ball."

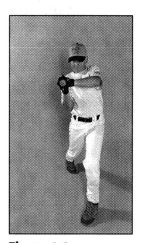  

Figure 4-1

What does "staying inside the ball" really mean?

"Staying inside the ball" is just one of the "cues" coaches use to restrain the hitter from letting his hands get away from his body in the swing. Two other fairly common "cues" used by coaches are "knob (and/or hands) to the ball," and "hit the 'inside half' of the ball."

Let's review some key points for a second. We know high bat velocity is produced through the "kinetic link," where energy generation begins at the feet and is sequentially transferred up through the legs, hips, shoulders, arms, and hands. This energy increases successively until it is maximized at the end of the bat, resulting in unparalleled angular velocity. What's important to understand in this instance, is that high bat velocity comes from these "linked" body segments.

The kinetic link works *in conjunction* with the hands staying inside the ball, which means the hands and bat remain close to the body during upper body rotation. For this to occur, the rear elbow MUST tuck in on the approach (refer to Figure 4-1). The hand path stays circular until the hips begin to decelerate and the torso has received its maximum momentum transfer. The hands then fire straight forward to extend "through" the ball. This occurs as the swing nears the appropriate contact zone, and is dependent on pitch location. Extension occurs as the swing nears the appropriate contact zone, which is dependent on pitch location

The hands and bat travel in a tight circular movement as they follow the rotating upper body, with the barrel dropping *below* the hands on the approach to contact. The bat head will *always* be below the hands at contact—unless the player swings at a pitch above his letters—at which point the barrel of the bat *could* be higher than his hands as he attempts to get on the plane of the pitch.

Why is "staying inside the ball" so important? Staying inside the ball keeps the hitter "short" to the ball, maximizes bat quickness and bat velocity, supports the hands at extension, and gives us more "time" to look pitches over! We'll explore these in more depth as we go along.

We've all seen figure skaters performing either in person, or on television. When we see figure skaters attempting to "spin" while remaining in one place, we see clearly the laws of physics in action. Like spinning figure skaters, who turn fastest when their arms are close to their bodies, batters likewise need to keep their arms as "close" to them as possible.

This factor also creates the fastest and most powerful spin during the swing. Here's why. When you watch figure skaters

Photo credit: Steve Powell/Allsport

spin with their arms outstretched and horizontal to the ground, they're not able to spin very fast—there's just too much drag. As they bring their hands and arms together, over their heads, their spinning rate increases. But, when they subsequently bring their hands down and in, to their chests, their spinning rate is maximized. In physics, this is called the "law of conservation of angular momentum," which simply put, means a rotating body will continue to spin at its maximum velocity—for as long as possible—as long as nothing encumbers, interferes, or gets in its way. In the skaters' case, this would be their arms protruding out from their rotating body's axis. The previous chapter reviewed the fact that the legs control hip rotation, and the hips determine the speed of the swing. If we set this up correctly in the swing, it will become undone in an instant, if the hitter casts his hands away from his body on the move to impact.

The "Pinball" Machine

Another example that makes sense—because we've all played them—are pinball machines. The path of the hands in the baseball swing should be the SAME for all pitches. In a pinball game, the bat "swivel" is immovable. We can't shift the hands to the ball; we have to "time" it correctly to hit it well. To hit an oncoming pinball that is "away," we must let it get deep, or we "run out of bat"—we can't reach it, or hit it off the end. Conversely, if we perceive the pinball to be "inside," we must meet it out in front—we can't let it get deep, or we get jammed. *The arc of the pinball-bat swing doesn't change; we're just making contact at different points in that swing-arc.* If we move our hands "to" the ball that is away (outside), essentially we're casting our hands and arms— losing bat speed, lengthening the swing, and hitting around the ball. Getting into an "unsupported' position like this does absolutely nothing for bat quickness or power. Many times you will read in newspapers struggling players saying, "I've got to let the ball get to me." Yet, so many players who come to me for instruction tell me their coach has told them to "go out and get the outside pitch." "Let it get deep" is a cue that I consider to be one of the good ones.

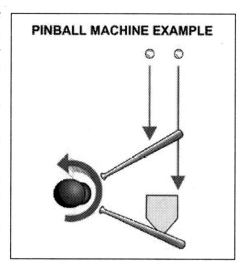

PINBALL MACHINE EXAMPLE

As we can see, if the pitch is middle-half in, we've got to get the head of the bat out in front. If we don't, we can't get extended—we get jammed. This is why good mechanics, coupled with depth perception and timing, are so critical to a hitter, and why the personal "resources" we are born with are so valuable if the hitter is to hit his potential.

How and Where Do These Casting Symptoms Start?

In my opinion, there are many reasons that I can think of. The first concerns youngsters who are asked to cover a regulation-size plate (17" width) with their short arms and bats. For a youngster to be able to do this, he almost has to stand on top of the *inside* corner of the plate. Couple this with younger players and the ever-present "fear" factor, and, well, you can see that this makes for a group of hitters who stand far off the plate and largely contribute to "diving" and "casting." By the time these players mature, they have either made the proper adjustments, or need a swing makeover, ostensibly to correct these symptoms. We must remember *there is a direct correlation between arm length, bat length, and proximity to the plate*. We violate this correlation all time. We shouldn't. But, we do.

Aluminum bats and the linear swing have escalated our awareness to this hitting malady. While I remember hitters talking about "keeping the hands in" when I played in the big leagues from the middle '60s to the middle '70s, this problem grew to grandiose proportions AFTER the advent of the aluminum bat. Players taught to hit with level shoulders during this period, and/or to swing down, have also been taught to keep their rear elbows "up." And, in the swing, we have an "either/or" relationship set up with the elbows. If the rear elbow stays up in the swing, the front elbow *must* work down. If the front elbow works down, we swing down. And vice versa. We can't hit with both elbows up—or both elbows down! And, if the rear elbow doesn't "tuck in" on the swing's approach, the hands will naturally work AWAY from the body, also. Good lower body, rotational hitting, however, precludes this from happening, because the rear elbow must tuck in to allow the lead elbow to work up. The hands naturally rotate around the body to the incoming pitch. A rotational hitter can "feel" the difference in his swing. If his hands cast out, his bat feels like it has a parachute on it! (Remember the figure skaters?) The "bad" news is he has "no" swing at this point; the "good" news is he can *self-correct*, because he knows it doesn't "feel" right! The linear hitter is not quite as fortunate, and is just one of the reasons why linear hitting is on its way out, and rotational hitting is returning.

Hitters have also gotten into this casting move by emulating ML hitters they see on television. While I am a big advocate of emulation as a teaching tool, it can also lead a hitter down an unforgiving path if not used with discretion. At times, we see some good ML players that "bar" (pre-extend) their lead arms, or cock their bottom wrists. So, since they do it, it must be right. Well, we also see *more* players who *don't* bar their lead arm, but since we see some that do, we tend to copy it. However, in my experience, most amateur players who keep their lead arms pre-extended in the launch position tend to hit "around the ball" more than those who maintain "soft" elbows throughout the swing, until extension.

Many times, they are also "late" at contact. They're late because the barrel of their bat has further to go until contact, creating a longer swing. I'm simply stating my experience working with hitters, as are others who may have differing viewpoints. Most big leaguers make on-the-fly adjustments to pitches that many others cannot—especially on a consistent basis. Because they have the "resources" to do it, they're baseball's best! No one in recent memory bars his lead arm at the launch position to the extent that Julio Franco does, yet he is a terrific hitter. At the launch position, the barrel of his bat is high over his head, pointing BACK at the pitcher! His own personal assets allowed him to hit that way. But, if you were an instructor, would you teach your son/daughter or other budding players to copy him? Probably not. For every Franco and those *few* that can do it, there are probably a jillion hitters we never heard of because they DID this very same thing—and got nowhere! The arm to watch, however, is the rear one: if this extends too quickly, the player is left with little choice but to hit around the ball. The back elbow must ultimately tuck in if we are to stay inside the ball!

Sadly, many players have suffered from poor coaching. No one admires and respects the hard work and dedication all coaches put into teaching young hitters more than I. Many of my best friends are coaches. However, the resources for coaches to find good, usable, teachable information, is very difficult to find. Rod Dedeaux, the legendary University of Southern California baseball coach (seven CONSECUTIVE N.C.A.A. championships) regrettably told me, "I'm convinced, after over 60 years of coaching, more good players never realize their dream because of poor coaching, rather than a lack of ability."

And some "cues" have hindered more than helped—cues like "separate your hands from your body" and "walk away from your hands." When a hitter does this, he automatically extends his lead arm, as his hands go rearward. He's already barred his lead arm! Very few players can vindicate themselves from this difficult start. And, how about "center the bat?" This cue puts the barrel-end of the bat angled back towards the pitcher, positioned over the button on the player's cap—and often times beyond. This is accomplished, in the pre-swing, by "cocking" the bottom wrist. Teachers of this cue "justify" it by saying it seems to give hitters a little more bat speed, and therefore, power. But, it also produces a "longer" swing, making timing much more difficult, and, if the hitter doesn't get his back elbow tucked back in on his approach, he'll cast his hands out into an unsupported position, reducing his power potential. For me, as an instructor, the trade-off isn't worth it. Timing is the name of the game!

My experience is younger players really struggle with this. If a player is taught "good" rotational mechanics, like those in my video, he should NATURALLY stay inside the ball. I personally find soft elbows work for me, from stance through pre-swing through approach. At contact is where BOTH elbows/arms should extend THROUGH the ball. I want my players to be compact and "short to the ball," which is another way of saying "stay inside the ball." Cocking the bottom wrist, producing a pre-extension of the lead arm at the launch position, makes for a much "longer" and less powerful swing. IMO, something to be avoided early-on.

We All Need Support!

When we cast our hands, yet another problem occurs: they never get "supported" by our body at contact. One of the benefits of the rotational swing is the player has his hands supported by his body.

In fact, a hitter's "length of stroke" is minimized when he lets the outside pitch get "deep." It's one reason why hitters hit fewer home runs to the opposite field. They can't generate enough momentum at this point in their swing. Another reason is the position of their hands at point of contact; they aren't totally supported by the body. Contact happens too "soon" after launching the swing. On the other hand, when we hit the ball out in front of our lead knee, on pitches middle-half in, our hands follow our body's rotation to the point where they extend through the ball, out in *front* of the hitter's body. In this position, the player's body supports his hands.

When a player like Mark McGwire, weighing 260 pounds, with a 91-mph bat speed, hands supported by his body, and a low center of gravity, swings—well, you can see why he has the power he does. There's NO "give" in his hands or arms at contact. But, even smaller players who show terrific power, get their hands in the same advantaged position.

Players who cast their hands and hit around the ball lose the advantage of their bodies lending support to their hands. I read a report a few years ago that said 42 out of the top 50 homerun hitters in ML history weighed *less* than 190 lbs. Staying inside the ball is one of the contributors to this amazing statistic.

Why Can't I Swing a Heavier Bat?

I get asked this question daily, now that high school players, like their college brethren, must use the new minus 3 bats. When aluminum bats were -5 or lighter (up to -12s!), a hitter could use "just" his hands and arms in the swing. He didn't need his lower body to be effective, and he didn't need to keep his hands inside the ball. The aluminum bat did all the work! Minus 3s preclude that from happening. Minus 3s are like wood bats. If players are to swing them effectively, they must start using mechanics that correctly incorporate good lower body mechanics into their swing. And, with good, lower-body rotational mechanics, a player "naturally" will keep his hands inside the ball. When the hands are unsupported, because they are casting away from the body, it induces us to use lighter bats. We all know the example of a person being able to hold a heavy weight for a longer period of time if he holds the weight close to his body. If he moves the same weight directly out, away from him in outstretched arms, he can't hold the weight nearly as long. It's too heavy. The same holds true for a hitter. When he casts his hands away from his body, the weight of his bat also *includes the weight of his arms!* It's just too much to overcome. Light aluminum bats over the years have lulled hitters into hands and arms mechanics. For those looking to get to the next "level," the "moment of truth" is now upon us.

Keeping Pitches "Fair"

Hitting around the ball also keeps players from hitting good pitches fair! A few years ago, the San Diego Padres had a marvelous player in Steve Finley, a player whom they had traded for from the Houston organization. He came to San Diego as a contact hitter, with little power. But, as he made his adjustments from being a swing-down, linear hitter to a lower-body, rotational hitter and began to get his "hips to lead his hands," he became a 30+ home run guy for the Padres. He became a real productive force on the Padres' good teams a few years back. Then, he got into a bad habit. He started pre-extending his lead elbow and hitting around the ball. Well, pitchers noticed this, too, and started giving him "hittable" fastballs middle-half in, early in the count. Well, as he should, he "jumped" on these pitches and hit 'em all over 400'—but FOUL! Now, he was behind in the count 0-2 or 1-2, and after having his bat "sped up" by inside cheese, they threw him off-speed pitches out away from him, trying to pick up

Photo credit: Todd Warshaw/Allsport

Steve Finley — Notice "barred" lead arm and pre-extended rear elbow.

the outside corner. Steve hit half the home runs as the year before and probably led the NL in 4-3 groundouts that year. The Padres felt he was "slowing down" and let him go to the Arizona Diamondbacks, via free agency. Finley corrected his casting, stayed inside the ball, and hit 36 home runs the next year for Arizona.

If the arms do extend too early, they will cause the hands and bat to travel in a wide circular path. When this happens out in front, the bat approaches the ball more from the side, which severely limits the player from exposing the entire "sweet spot" of his bat to the oncoming pitch. And, he has to hit the pitch so far out in front (so he won't get jammed), that he loses the precious moments when he could be deciding whether it is a good pitch to hit.

Harry Heilmann, the Hall of Fame outfielder for the Detroit Tigers in the '20s—who hit over .400 twice in his career—said he went from being a "good" hitter to a "great" hitter, when he learned how to inside-out the fastball on the *inside* corner—when he had two strikes on him. This is a wonderful piece of information for all hitters. What he was telling us was that by being able to keep his bat 90° to the oncoming pitch on the inside corner, he was able to hit the ball back through the pitcher.

When we think about it, we can see exactly what he was saying. We can ONLY do this by doing two things: 1) by keeping our hands inside the ball, and 2) by using good lower-body, rotational mechanics, whereby the hands have the ability to wrap around the rotating body, as the arms extend toward the pitcher. This produces the inside-out swing. When a hitter is able to do this, he picks up more TIME—the elusive commodity hitters never seem to have enough of. And, with two strikes, he doesn't have to be as "conscious" of the inside fastball—he can wait longer—which then makes hitting the off-speed and breaking pitches much easier. It worked in Heilmann's day—and it's still working today. Rotational mechanics are for real.

Can You Give Us ONE Current Big League Example Who Does This "Right?"

You bet I can! Take a look at the ML's best hitters, and you'll see it in action daily. You don't become great NOT doing it correctly. But, if I had to pick ONE player, I'd tell you that Edgar Martinez of the Seattle Mariners is a "clinic" in motion. He inside-outs the ball, in my opinion, as well—or better—than anyone I can ever remember seeing. He's some kind of hitter!

Edgar Martinez—notice the correct position of his rear elbow, close to his body.

Okay, Mike, You've "Sold" Me. Is There a Drill I Can Teach/Learn?

In my hitting video, "Do We Teach What We Really See?", I demonstrate one of my proprietary drills that have given many hitters new "leases" on their careers. I call it the "fence" drill (as do many others). However, mine differs in that I place the hitter next to the fence much closer than the conventional fence drills. Conventional fence drills place the hitter a bat's length away from the fence. Mine places the hitter 12-13" from the fence. I do this because I want to make the player "work" to understand how the hands really work in the swing. If it's made too easy for him, his muscle memory doesn't burn in, and the message sent to his body is not as clear-cut and meaningful. In the off-season, agents often send me professional players to correct a mechanical problem and "jump start" their careers. I've put these players up against the fence this way, and they refuse to swing. "It can't be done," they say, shaking their heads. But, after a couple of days, they're amazed that they do it. Once they have it mastered, they begin to realize just how restraining it's been for both them and their careers. But, a drill like this isn't something you do once or twice. Hitting is a discipline, and must be continually worked on. It's a never-ending work in progress.

Can You Leave Us with One "Tip" We Can Use?

Many times I see hitters with good rotational mechanics who properly tuck their rear elbows in, don't cock their bottom wrists, and don't separate their hands from their bodies, yet still wind up pre-extending and barring the front arm. This can be confusing to the instructor and player alike, and very difficult to correct. As we learned earlier, when the front heel drops to initiate hip rotation, the "explosion" is so violent, that many times, if no tension is placed on the lead arm, it will leave the hands "back" for a split second. And, this will cause the lead arm to straighten out—and make it appear that the hitter has barred his front arm—when, in reality, he's done everything correct up to that point! So, the one tip I will leave you with is to remember to put a little "tension" on the lead arm in the stance. What's important here is the hands, arms, and upper body go back as a "unit," keeping the elbows "soft." Correctly "anchoring" the front arm at this position can be one of hardest mechanical movements to master. But, once mastered, it will pay the hitter back in "spades."

The Need for Staying "Up-to-Date"

We teach what we hear, or what we read, or what WE were taught when we played, rather than staying "up-to-date" with the latest goings-on. Hitting has changed drastically over the past few years—and will continue to do so with the introduction of the new minus 3 bats. We see this change daily with baseball's "new" cue: "stay back." We can all remember just a few short years ago when everyone was teaching players to "load up" and then get their weight to the *front side*. Today, it's 180° the other way! This is confusing to coaches and hitters alike. We need to teach things that are logical, make sense, are not faddish—and are up-to-date! The minus 3s are finally *making* us zero in on the mechanics used by 95% of baseball's Hall of Fame hitters. My intent with these articles is to hopefully provide this information so as many people as possible can hit "their" potential—coaching wise AND performance wise.

By this time, I hope I've made my points clear: "staying inside the ball" is one of my three "core" mechanics" because of the positive effects it has on high OPS. And one of the three reasons why 10% of the players make 90% of the money. It's worth getting it right!

PART II

Ask Mike Epstein

CHAPTER 5

"I'm Making Contact, But Have Little or No Power"

The introduction of the minus 3 aluminum bats at the high school and collegiate levels have noticeably increased the number of emails I receive addressing this particular question. In addition, since 1995, hitting mechanics have changed dramatically, further popularizing this question. Slugging percentages have continued their downward spiral since the minus 3s came on the scene. And while, in my opinion, it has effectively addressed a serious problem with the amateur game, it has caused concern from parents, coaches, and players alike. "My son (players) used to hit for power. What gives?" The "heavier" bats have greatly contributed to this increasing awareness of diminished power.

It seems everyone wants "more" power for various and particular reasons. Many are looking for the "right formula," feeling power can take them to the next level. And, in some cases, it can.

Hitting for power can take on various connotations, depending on the hitter's "type." There is "line-drive" power, "gap" power, and "over-the-fence" power. Dealing with as many different hitters as I do, power ultimately becomes a "type" issue. Allow me to explain.

Rather than asking WHY a hitter doesn't have power, a much better question might be WHAT "type" hitter is he? Answering this question objectively and HONESTLY can make a huge difference in the player reaching his individual potential. Most parents want their sons to be power hitters, and coaches are always looking for three or four big hitters in the middle of the lineup. And, the players themselves seem to identify more with the Mark McGwires and Ken Griffeys of the baseball world, than players' "other" types. But, honestly, few fit in that class.

I group hitters into three hitting "type" categories: singles/contact hitters, line-drive gap hitters, and true home run hitters. Fifteen percent of hitters will fall into singles/contact hitters, 70% in the line-drive gap hitter group, and 15% will be true home run hitters. We have to know WHO the hitter is, and WHICH group he fits into, before we can address the question of "WHY doesn't he hit for more power?"

And to deal effectively with this issue, coaches/hitters should realize that, because of these hitting "types," some players can never achieve the power numbers of others. These players normally have other attributes that make them extremely valuable to overall offensive output. They make contact, steal bases, move runners along, and "set the table" for the 3-4-5-6 hitters in the lineup. While power is important in a balanced lineup, answering this question should in no way denigrate the importance of those players who may not be blessed with big-time power potential. There is a vital role for these players—on every team.

However, it should be noted, *ALL players have the POTENTIAL for more production with a proper hitting approach and a good hitting "plan" when they go to the plate!* For those who do possess this elusive commodity, but aren't showing it, there are some remedies which I have found very effective. If you've read my articles or watched my videos, you know the importance I place on not only the mechanical side, but also the mental side. But, in order to answer this question, I am going to identify some key areas, in the form of a checklist, where the hitter can potentially go awry. This mental checklist enables me to spot where the problems may lie that can materially affect the player's power potential.

A very important point to remember is to "zero in" on the player's universal "technique," rather than his personal "style." The only time I correct a player's personal "style" is if it restrains him from getting to the proper launch position—on time. If his style allows him to do this, his problem invariably lies in the area from stride to launch to contact. In other words: his technique. Noted University of Hawaii baseball coach, Coop DeRenne, said it best: "Treat the illness-technique—not the stylistic symptom!"

❏ *Does the player have a firm grip on the bat?* This is often overlooked, but an important item to consider. The player's top-hand grip should be in his fingers, while his bottom-hand grip should be in the "crotch" of his hand. "Not too light and not too tight," but firm.

❏ *Are his knuckles lined up correctly?* Aligning the knuckles also seems to be a part of hitting that doesn't garner too much attention. But, it really deserves a closer look, because not gripping the bat correctly, (i.e., "wrapping" his top hand) can cause the hitter to "cast" and hit around the ball, severely limiting his ability to hit effectively middle-half in, and reducing his power potential.

I teach the bat grip in a very easy-to-understand way. I ask the player, holding the bat handle, to place the bat, barrel down, between his feet. I ask him to take his hands off the bat and "lean" it against his body. Then, I ask him to pick the bat up by the handle, with both hands. This automatically places his hands in the correct grip: the "knocker" knuckles of the top hand will be aligned perfectly BETWEEN the "knocker" knuckles and the big knuckles on his bottom hand. Try it. It's a no-brainer!

❑ *Is the player separating his hands from his body in the stride ?* (Refer to Figure 5-1, A.) In rotational hitting, separating the hands from the body too far, in the stride, will induce the player to hit around the ball, sapping power dramatically. If his hands go back too far, his lead elbow begins to straighten. It is very difficult, especially for younger players, to stay inside the ball with a lead arm that has "barred out." The player's upper half (torso, hands, and arms) should counter-rotate as a "unit."

❑ *Is the player opening his front foot "enough" to allow the hips to get through?* (Refer to Figure 5-1, B.) If the front foot doesn't open up to at least 45°, it is extremely difficult for the hips to "get through." If the hips can't get through to "lead the hands" to the ball, the player is left with a hands/arms swing. A significant part of hitting for power is using the "big muscles" (legs) of the body to do most of the work. As the player opens his front foot, watch for his upper torso to be counter-rotating back. This MUST happen to create the proper torquing action.

❑ *Is the player balanced when he launches his swing?* (Refer to Figure 5-1, C.) Most players are taught that "balance" is good, something to strive for when hitting. And, I agree. Unfortunately, we don't define "balance" for the player, nor tell him "how" to be balanced in the swing. "Dynamic" balance is something to shoot for, from launch to contact to follow-through.

Watch for the player who does NOT re-gain the balance point in his stride! (Refer to Figure 5-1, B.) When the player is balanced, there is an ultra-smooth transition from one hitting sequence to the next. When this happens, the transfer of maximum energy, from back to blocked front side (linear to angular) and from bottom to top (kinetic), is optimized. And another important item to remember is that rotational hitting *implies* balance, meaning that it is impossible to rotate correctly on one leg. If we "sit" on our back leg, we "spin," instead of rotating. If our weight goes to our front side (lunging), it is almost impossible to rotate at all, and we become "hands and arms hitters." So, *make sure the hitter is balanced when his hips "pop!"*

❑ *Is the player dropping his heel before launching his swing?* (Refer to Figure 5-1, C.) The hips are initiated in the stride with the FRONT foot! If the player's front heel doesn't "drop," he has nothing to initiate his hip rotation, or "trigger" his swing. I've always been amazed at the answers I get from both amateur and professional players when I ask them, "Do you know what triggers your swing?" When the front heel drops, this singular movement initiates the hips, leading to the torque position. Make sure the hitter doesn't launch his swing before the front heel drops.

Figure 5-1. 17-year-old (pure power-type hitter)

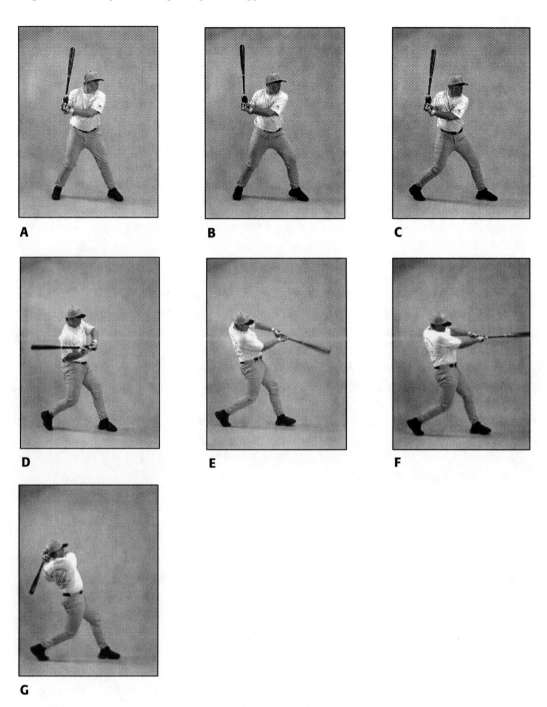

A

B

C

D

E

F

G

❑ *Is the player getting to the proper "torque position?"* (Refer to Figure 5-1, C.) The torque position is the "separation" of the upper and lower body parts, and is the root for maximizing bat speed, bat quickness, and power in the swing. Is the hitter getting there (top half "closed," bottom-half "open")? When I evaluate a player's body positioning, I look for the front foot to be open (45°-90°) and check to see if the player's hips are "leading" his hands to the ball. If he's "torquing" his body correctly (I call this "winding the rubber band"), I move on to other checkpoints. Note: This is a KEY point on the checklist!

❑ *Is the player hitting "around the ball?"* (Refer to Figure 5-1, C-D.) To optimize bat quickness from launch to contact, the player must stay inside the ball. In rotational hitting, this means the hands follow his rotating body around the axis from launch to contact to follow-through. As a result, "staying inside the ball" becomes a natural movement. It is far more difficult to do this if the lower body doesn't rotate, and is one of the principal reasons why "hitting around the ball" has been so topical since the advent of the aluminum bat and linear hitting.

❑ *Is the player rolling his wrists at contact?* (Refer to Figure 5-1, D-E.) The wrists represent one of the weakest muscle groups in the body. Why make them "weaker" by rolling them at contact? A strong impact position implies that the wrists must roll well AFTER contact. In the contact position, the player's palms should be "flat," parallel to the ground, and unbroken (the degree of flatness will depend on contact location). (Refer to Figure 5-1, E-G.) Players who demonstrate a wrist-roll at contact are players who have been taught to swing down through the ball. You can easily try this by picking up a bat and swinging down. You can experience how easy it is to roll your wrists at contact by effectuating this. Now, give your swing a slight upslope, as in a "natural" swing, and see where your wrists "break." You'll find that in this latter position, they will break somewhere out behind your ear.

❑ *Is the player staying on the axis of rotation that he set up in the stride?* (Refer to Figure 5-1, A-G.) As stated earlier, the player MUST re-gain the "balance point" in his stride! Staying on the axis of rotation that the player sets up in his stride is crucial to maximizing the player's rotational velocity. Like a spinning top, if the player strays off the axis too far, his rotational velocity decreases. A "yawing" top loses velocity rapidly and falls over. What style hitter a player is should determine where he aligns himself on the axis. A power hitter will be back off the axis somewhat (refer to Figure 5-1, E), the line-drive gap hitter not as far, and the singles/contact hitter should be right on it. The player who sits too far forward (negative) on the axis will have a very difficult time reaching his power potential. Where the player sits on the axis ordinarily determines the type hitter he is, because this positioning sets his bat path during the swing: a steeper gradient for the home-run hitter and a more level swing gradient for the line-drive/ground-ball hitter. Too far forward—or back—off the axis, however, will restrain the body from rotating at its maximum rotational potential. *Look for the player's hips to remain "level" from launch to contact to follow through.*

❑ *Is the player "anticipating" pitches correctly?* Does he have a hitting PLAN before getting into the batters' box? Anticipating pitches correctly, with less than two strikes, can do wonders for timing and power. If he "knows" a certain pitch is coming beforehand, and he already has a "reference" on that pitch, the player should be able to time it correctly. Getting a "head-start" like this is important. On the other hand, if the hitter waits to see what the pitch is before he commits (as in correct two-strike hitting), many times he will be a tad tardy on the fast ball, and a little early on the off-speed pitch. By anticipating correctly with less than two strikes, the hitter can take the element of "surprise" away from the pitcher, increasing his "dead-red" hitting area, and boosting his chances to hit the ball hard.

❑ *Is the player doing the torque, numbers, and fence drills™?* I have my own proprietary drills, that I demonstrate on Tape #2 of my videotape set, "Do We Teach What We Really See?" These are the same drills I use to "de-learn" and "re-learn" rotational hitting. Aside from the learning factor, these same drills also act to keep the player "in the envelope" during his season. If a player is diligent doing his drills during the season, chances are, if he does run into a problem, it won't be a mechanical one. At that point, we must focus on his thought process and his powers of concentration when he goes to the plate. Analyzing hitters is always a matter of subtraction, clarification, and the communication of timely, accurate information.

It is wise to keep in mind that not every player is capable of being a "true" power hitter, however much the parent/player/coach may want it. But, nearly every player, with good, rotational mechanics and a solid "plan" when he goes to the plate, is capable of hitting the ball harder. And having timely, accurate information for an analysis, as in a "checklist," can go a long way in determining the problem and helping the hitter realize his own, individual "power" potential.

CHAPTER 6

"I Can't Stop Lunging and Coming Forward When I Swing!"

This hitting problem gets a lot of "play" these days. It is so topical because of what we have been teaching hitters over the past 25 years or so. Since the advent of the aluminum bat and Astroturf playing fields in the early '70s, we have been instructing players to hit with their hands and arms, transfer their weight back to front, and come forward. We have players, coaches, instructors, and parents who have literally "cut their eye teeth" learning to hit with the aluminum bat and its associated linear-type mechanics. "Coming forward" has been ingrained in us for a long enough period of time to a point where changing over to something "else" can become difficult, and sometimes, awkward, to both player and coach. But, in reality, overcoming this problem is really just a matter of good information and the motivation to succeed.

We know hitting is changing, because questions similar to the one I'm tackling here reflect this transition. Today, the "buzzword" is "stay back"—not "come forward"—as in the past two and one-half decades. And, as we think about this transition, we begin to realize that big changes are already underway—as much as 180° in the opposite direction!

While there are many coaches working hard to facilitate this transition within their programs, there are still too many who resist making these timely changes, or perhaps, may be confused how to go about it. I hear coaches yelling "stay back" to their hitters, but they still continue with the buzzwords attendant to the linear hitting mechanics with which they are familiar. Every time we ask a hitter to keep his shoulders "level," essentially, we are really asking him to "come forward." And every time we ask a hitter to swing "level" or "down," basically, we are asking him to "come forward." Unfortunately for the hitter, correct biomechanical movements and physics make it virtually impossible for the player to keep his weight "back," and also to swing "down," or swing "level." Please don't misunderstand what I'm saying here. It CAN be done, but it won't feel "right" or look "fluid," or in most cases yield a high OPS. As I travel around the country speaking to groups of coaches and players, it is apparent the level of frustration and confusion that has set in with both groups.

It's important for us to remember that each hitting system has its own "laws." We need to keep each system intact, whichever "system" you choose for your player(s) or team. Combining different hitting "systems" creates confusion—and makes a very tough task, much tougher.

But, while the change is already in place at the major league level, we are significantly lagging in the minor leagues and amateur ball. We're still teaching "level" shoulders, swinging down, and "keeping the bat head above the hands." These actions contribute to lunging, which quickly dissipates bat speed and power. And, I believe this is the primary reason why so many players and coaches are preoccupied with curtailing "coming forward" and "lunging."

Once again, I have put together a "checklist" for you. This is the same mental checklist I use when working with hitters who display this hitting symptom. Hopefully, one or more of these key points will be able to shed more light on the things to look for and some useful ways to correct it.

❑ *Is the player doing his drills?* If the player is one of "my" former students—and he tells me he is coming forward and lunging—the very FIRST question I ask him is, "Are you doing your drills?" It happens very infrequently, but there are a few players who "think" they've got a hold on these good mechanics when they leave me. Sometime later, they run into a problem like this. In every instance, they tell me they didn't think they had to do the drills any more. Nothing could be further from the truth! Once a player learns good mechanics, he must continually work on them until the last time he puts on his spikes. Hitting is the toughest thing to do in sports, yet, in many cases, we treat it as if it's as easy as "blinking." My mentor, Ted Williams, said "the natural hitter has worked longer and harder than any player on the field." After all these years of playing and teaching, I know he was right. While some things in hitting may vary down through the years, this singular part of hitting won't change. If you want it, you've got to work it.

In my videotape ("Do We Teach What We Really See?"), the drills I use to teach proper rotational mechanics also are designed to keep the player "in the envelope" after he completes his instruction. All it takes is a few swings each day to ensure this problem of coming forward and lunging never comes back. It's certainly worth the small effort. Once the player starts using the drills again, the problem goes away.

❑ *Is the player balanced when he launches his swing?* (Refer to Figure 6-1, A-C.) Balance is one of the overriding conditions in a correct swing. The goal of every instructor/player should be a "repeatable" swing, and balance is a prerequisite for this condition. If the player is balanced, his weight should not come forward. A common "cue" used today by coaches is "load up." We teach this because we are trying to get our players to "stay back"—not "come forward," which was yesterday's buzzword. I find that if the player loads up—and doesn't regain the balance point in his stride, the amount of weight he holds on his back side will flow in an equal amount to his front side as he swings, sustaining the lunging condition. Balance means 50-50. For the player not to lunge, he MUST regain the balance point in his stride, and be balanced when he launches his swing.

❏ *Is the player keeping his back leg bent when he strides and drops his heel?* (Refer to Figure 6-1, C.)If the player's back leg (knee) is not at a 90° angle, chances are he is pushing forward when he swings. Check to see that his rear thigh is perpendicular to the ground. If it's tilted forward, he's lunged, and his weight will go to the inside of his front thigh. An important point to remember, though, is 90° is only a coaching truism, not a mechanical truism. If a player swings at a pitch "up" in the zone, he may come forward somewhat, increasing the 90° angle as he flattens out his swing to match the plane of the pitch. The same is true on a pitch "down;" the player may "tilt" rearward more to match the pitch plane and decrease the 90° figure a little. Proper on-the-fly adjustments are a necessary part of hitting. Keen observation is a must.

❏ *Is the player's back leg bent when he drops his heel?* (Refer to Figure 6-1, C-D.)This movement is consistent with the "tilting" movement elaborated in a subsequent checkpoint. A cue I use is to tell the player that he should "feel" a rope—stretched tight—running from his front heel to his rear shoulder. When the player drops his front heel, the imaginary "rope" should "pull down" his rear shoulder, as his front heel drops.

❏ *Is the player's rear elbow tucking in as he launches his swing?* (Refer to Figure 6-1, C-D.) If his rear elbow stays up when he launches his swing, the only way his lead elbow can work is down; we can't hit with BOTH elbows up. And, if his lead elbow works down, his shoulders will remain "relatively" level, his swing will be level to down, and his weight will come forward.

❏ *Is the player "tilting" correctly and getting his lead elbow up in time?* (Refer to Figure 6-1, C-D.) This is one of the key points to look for! This singular movement can stop linear movement dead in its tracks! When the player's front heel drops, his rear shoulder must begin to dip at nearly the same instant. As this is happening, the player's rear elbow must begin to tuck in close to his body, allowing his lead elbow to begin working up. This "tilting" movement will automatically place the player's weight to the INSIDE of his rear thigh, precluding any forward movement.

❏ *Is the player "sitting down" on top of his rear leg in the approach?* (Refer to Figure 6-1, D.) Obviously, if the player is doing this, he "won't" be able to come forward. Unless he's "Spiderman," his body can only go one way at a time!

Figure 6-1. 13-year-old (Line/Drive Gap-Type Hitter)

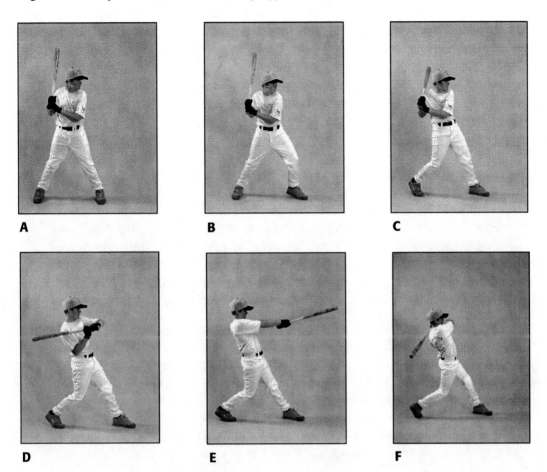

A   B   C

D   E   F

❑ *Is the player straightening his front knee as he drops his front heel?* (Refer to Figure 6-1, C-E.) There are many areas in the swing where "torque" comes into play. Once again, a simple definition of "torque" is two forces working in opposite directions on an object. In this case, as the hitter is starting his swing (forward movement of the lower body and trailing upper torso), his front knee begins to straighten out, beginning an opposite, rearward movement. This torquing provides "leverage" in the swing, helping to bring the trailing bat head to the impact position, producing an ultra-high, angular bat velocity. It also keeps the hitter's rotating body from coming forward, because as the front heel drops to initiate the swing, the front leg begins to straighten, and helps "block" the front side from coming forward. This blocking action keeps the body rotating around the axis and impedes any forward or lunging movements. So, keep an eye on the front knee. You should see this ultra-rapid, reflexive action in the lead knee, from bent to "rigid" to bent. But watch closely. It takes place in milliseconds!

❏ *Is the player controlling his stride length—striding too far?* (Refer to Figure 6-1, A-B.) The trend in hitting, today, is a short or no-stride approach, one which I personally subscribe to. The purposes of the stride are four-fold: 1) to break inertia (get the body moving and provide "rhythm" to the swing), 2) to aid "timing," 3) to set up an axis of rotation (for the body to rotate around), and 4) to regain the balance point. Contrary to popular belief, the length of a player's stride is NOT directly related to power potential, but striding "too far" can facilitate and enhance the player's linear movement forward.

Other Thoughts

Sometimes, in our quest to correct the hitter, we fail to notice where the pitch location is. This is especially true while studying videos. Even with first-rate rotational mechanics, there can/will be forward movement on pitches that are "up" in the strike zone. In order for the hitter to "match the plane of his swing to the plane of the pitch," he will/should automatically flatten out his swing to hit the high pitch. As a result, the knowledgeable instructor will notice a less pronounced "tilting" to the player's swing. If the pitch is high enough, even a proficient rotational hitter will come forward somewhat (and may even drag his rear foot) as his shoulders level off to match the pitch's plane.

On the other hand, the coach should see a much more pronounced "tilting" of the player's body—with no forward movement—if the pitch is down in the zone. We must also keep in mind that the mechanically efficient hitter is continually making instinctive, on-the-fly adjustments to the incoming pitch. But, this is entirely different from the player who comes forward *regardless* of pitch location. In many cases, he's been programmed to do this since he was a youngster. Cues such as "keep your shoulders level," swing "level" or "down," and "keep your lead elbow down" enhance and facilitate the lunging movement so many today are trying to change. Again, avoid "mixing" systems!

Hitting mechanics are undergoing a big metamorphosis today. To correct the common problem of "coming forward" and "lunging," one only needs, in most cases, to change the player's mechanics from linear to rotational. If taught correctly, this problem should quickly fade away.

CHAPTER 7

"I'm Always Swinging Late, Getting Jammed, and Popping Up"

Many players look for a mechanical answer to this problem, yet many times, the problem may be visual, or it could be mental. Often, we are late because we haven't done our "homework"—we have no "plan" when we go to the plate. As a result, we don't anticipate correctly—especially when the count is in our favor! However to answer this question, I will focus primarily on the role of mechanics and its impact on aiding the coach/player experiencing this problem.

When a hitter correctly matches the plane of his swing to the plane of the pitch, it makes diagnosing this problem decidedly simpler. If the hitter is matching the plane of his swing to the plane of the pitch, and he is late, he will hit the bottom half of the ball. My mentor, Ted Williams, in his own inimitable way, would always ask hitters, "Are you early—or late—when you pop the ball up?" He told me once that nearly every player he asked had given little, if any, thought to this question! And if hitters don't know if they are early or late, how are they going to make the proper adjustment(s) when they're in the batter's box? Many times, popping the ball up is indicative of being tardy to the contact zone, yet many coaches believe it is the product of an uppercut swing. Sometimes it is, but most times, the hitter is late.

From time immemorial, this hitting problem has persisted. But, I think that the transition from rotational mechanics to linear mechanics when the aluminum bats were introduced has had a lot to do with this problem becoming popular and topical. I can't begin to tell you just how many coaches/players/parents have asked me how to stop getting "jammed." Actually, way too many. With an aluminum bat, the hitter can still get jammed and hit the ball hard. This has given many hitters a false sense of having "good" mechanics and being "good" hitters. "Judgment Day" inevitably arrived when hitters had to swing a wood bat. If the player was late and didn't (couldn't) get his arms extended, the results were usually a broken bat and a handful of "bees." Simply, with a wood bat, the hitter has to be "right on" with every swing. With the aluminum bat and its spectacular resiliency—and huge "sweet spot," players with average talent and mechanics could have scintillating high school and college careers. Unfortunately, they had (and still have) rude awakenings when moving up to the professional level and the wood bat. Good mechanics can—and do—play a huge part in the orderly transition from metal to wood.

When I was with the Milwaukee Brewer organization in 1993, I told the "powers that be" that radical changes in hitting were on the horizon. Too many hitters couldn't hit the pitch in, or down and in, and they consistently got jammed. They scoffed at my suggestion to teach the players rotational mechanics, and wanted their hitters taught to stay "closed," to transfer their weight to the front side, and to swing down through the ball. This in spite of the fact that the Brewers' organization had one of the two lowest power indices in the minor leagues for a number of years. As the scenario unfolded, this changeover did begin by 1995, and we've been breaking offensive records ever since. Yet, unbelievably, these same linear mechanics are still being taught today by many amateur and professional coaches. But not so in the big leagues…. (yet another "story.")

Another question I get asked often by amateur players is do I think "practicing" with a wood bat will help a player. I tell them "yes and no." "Yes," because it teaches the hitter the "feel" of really getting jammed (ouch!). The player then realizes he can avoid this by taking remedial steps through adjustments (changes?)—or other ways to improve his hitting efficiency. And "no," in light of the recent introduction of the minus 3 aluminum bats, which closely simulate the weight/length ratio of wood bats, yielding a similar "feel" to both. And, minus 3s, hopefully, will get everyone on the "same" mechanics page. A minus 3 bat is a tough weight/length ratio to overcome without the proper use of good lower-body, rotational mechanics.

If you've seen my video tapes or read my articles, you are already aware of the history behind rotational mechanics and the profound effect they have had on productive hitting, so it is pointless to go through it again. Suffice to say that there is considerably less room for mistakes with the wood-bat, than with an aluminum one. However, rotational mechanics are easily adaptable to wood bat hitting because of the use of the total body in the swing. The same is not true with linear hitting, which is not readily adaptable to PRODUCTIVE hitting. These elements should be considered when instructing hitters and/or attempting to diagnose those who are continually late.

To more completely answer this question, I am going to identify some key areas, in the form of a written checklist, where the hitter can potentially go awry. For me, this mental checklist enables me to spot where the problems may lie that can materially affect the player's ability to get to the properly-timed contact location.

A very important point to remember is to "zero in" on the player's universal "technique," rather than his personal "style." The only time I correct a player's personal "style" is if it restrains him from getting to the proper launch position—on time. If his style allows him to do this, his problem invariably lies in the areas from stride to launch to contact. In other words: his technique. Former University of Hawaii baseball coach, Coop DeRenne, said it best: "Treat the illness-technique—not the stylistic-symptom!"

❑ *When did the hitter last get his eyes checked?* I know, this seems obvious and elementary, yet it seems that many times we overlook the obvious. You would be surprised how many hitting problems would be averted if the player could see optimally. My esteemed colleague and good friend, Dr. Bill Harrison (a nationally-recognized doctor of optometry who serves as a consultant to major league baseball teams), and I, were baseball teammates at the University of California (Berkeley) under George Wolfman, back in the "good ole days." Not too long ago, I remember Bill telling me that "the best mechanics in the world are useless if I put a blindfold on hitters." Of course, he is correct. So, don't overlook this important aspect when trying to determine why a hitter is continually late. This could (help) solve his problem. The hitter should have his eyes checked once a year by a competent eye doctor.

❑ *Is the hitter starting his counter-rotation before the pitcher releases the ball?* Starting on time should be one of hitting's "absolutes," but it seems few give it much consideration. Once a hitter is behind the "timing curve" on a pitch, it is normally impossible to catch up, and the hitter can't get his arms extended. To counteract this condition, the hitter should be starting his counter-rotation when the pitcher begins HIS counter-rotation. Too many times, we watch videos of hitters from the "open side," but disregard the view which includes both the pitcher and the hitter in the same clip. Make sure you take a few shots with both simultaneously in view. You'd be surprised at what you'll see! Many times, getting the hitter to simply "start on time" can remedy the problem all by itself!

❑ *Is the hitter striding at the right time?* There is no "set" time for the stride, but it normally coincides with the pitcher's throwing arm coming forward. It is purely personal and entirely dependent on the hitter's "makeup" and the total "resources" he has available on any given pitch. These personal resources include, but are not limited to, talent, ability, vision, and the quality of his mechanics. Hitters can also help themselves immeasurably by anticipating pitches correctly, based on the hitting "plan" they take to the plate with them.

❑ *Is the hitter dropping his front heel "on time?"* In rotational hitting, the hitter's front heel "triggers" his swing. If he doesn't get his front heel down on time, he has no "choice" but being late. This is another "personal" choice made by the hitter. Hitters with "poor" mechanics must start their swing earlier than those whose mechanics are short to the ball and compact. The front heel normally drops when the pitch is approximately 15' in front of the plate. I have an old clip of Babe Ruth taken from the top of an old rickety grandstand in St. Louis in the '20s, where he dropped his front heel when the oncoming pitch was about 10' in front of the plate and STILL pulled a line drive base hit between first and second! It's different for everyone—just make sure the heel gets down on time!

❏ *Is the hitter "cocking" his bottom wrist at the launch position?* (Refer to Figure 7-1, C.) Surprisingly, this is taught by some instructors. Their cue is "centering the bat." They feel this adds a few mph to the player's bat speed and some additional power through a torquing condition of the hands. I agree that this torquing condition is important, but it must be controlled, not allowing the bat head to come back over and past the head, and "point" back at the pitcher.

Hand torquing can still be accomplished with the bat head "perpendicular" to the ground at launch, which will shorten his swing by staying inside the ball, and appreciably increase his bat quickness to the contact zone. "Centering the bat" makes it much more difficult for the hitter to stay inside the ball. Here's why. As the bottom wrist begins to cock, it begins to straighten out the lead arm as well, leading to a premature "barring out" condition of the lead arm. This pre-extended, or barred-out condition, makes it very difficult to stay inside the ball on the approach. Personally, I would rather see a hitter sacrifice a few mph in bat speed and power to be able to stay inside and be "quick" to the point of contact. When it comes to hitting, TIMING IS THE NAME OF THE GAME. It's that important!

❏ *Is the hitter's front knee straightening as he drops his heel?* (Refer to Figure 7-1, C-G.) Rotational hitters make a reflexive movement "rearward" with their lead knee, as their swing comes forward. Doing so provides additional torque to the swing, facilitating two important movements: (1) in the approach phase, it provides additional "leverage," aiding in getting the bat head from its "lag" position to one of ultra-high angular velocity; (2) this "counter" movement of the lead knee also restrains the body's forward movement by inhibiting the hips from sliding forward before the hands start. If the player "bleeds" through this important blocking point in the swing (when the heel drops), he is relegated to lunging, and his hips will "slide," dissipating bat speed and bat quickness in a "heartbeat."

❏ *Is the bat too heavy?* There is no question that players who use their lower halves correctly can "shoulder" increased bat weights. Many times I am asked, "How heavy a bat should I swing?" I believe it's the longest and heaviest bat you can handle easily and *effectively*. The decision must be made by the hitter himself, based on his strength, size, experience, and the type of mechanics he uses. Rotational hitters who use the big muscles in their bodies (legs) effectively are normally predisposed to using a slightly bigger bat than their (hands/arms) linear counterparts. The additional length and weight contribute to more mass, leverage, and momentum which ultimately yield more power and production—ASSUMING THERE IS NO SIGNIFICANT LOSS OF BAT SPEED. If unsure, a hitter is best "erring" on the side of the slightly lighter, rather than heavier, bat. Bat quickness (launch to contact) and bat velocity, with a too-heavy bat, can be

Figure 7-1. 17-year-old (pure power-type hitter)

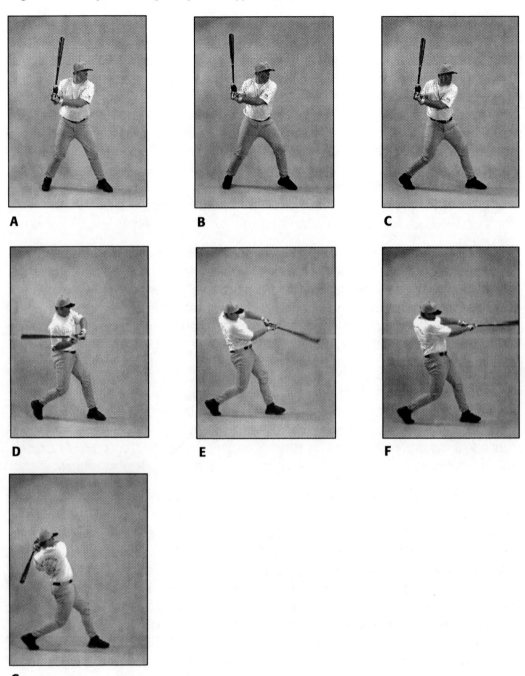

measurably reduced, resulting in being late (i.e., not being able to arrive at the predicted contact point on time).

❑ *Is the hitter staying inside the ball?* (Refer to Figure 7-1, D-G.) As most individuals who have read my articles know, staying inside the ball is one of my "core" mechanical movements. You've got to have it. If the hitter's hands are predisposed to hitting around the ball, he puts himself into the same category as the figure skater example previously cited in Chapter 3 and in my hitting videotape ("Do We Teach What We Really See?"). When a figure skater spins, he spins fastest when his arms are together, against his chest. He cannot spin very fast with outstretched arms. The same rule in physics applies to hitters: a rotating body cannot withstand the "encumbrance" of the hands and arms protruding away from its spinning axis. If this happens in the baseball swing, the body cannot rotate at its maximum rotational speed, resulting in decreased bat speed and quickness, and making it tougher to "arrive on time."

And, here's something else to consider and identify. When a player doesn't stay inside the ball, letting his hands drift away from his rotating body, he also offsets the sweet spot on his bat from its predicted contact area, further *away*. Accordingly, he simultaneously moves the handle of his bat closer to his predicted contact area, which results in the hitter often getting jammed. I hope I'm coming in loud and clear: staying inside the ball helps separate the prospects from the suspects by maximizing his bat quickness, and keeping the bat's sweet spot in the proper hitting area.

❑ *Is the hitter opening his front foot at least 45 degrees as he strides?* (Refer to Figure 7-1, B.) If the hitter's front foot remains closed in the swing, he blocks himself off from the inside pitch. Make sure his front foot opens in the stride, or he will continue to have trouble getting his hands through on time. And, you can bet pitchers will notice this and exploit it, until the hitter makes the appropriate adjustment.

❑ *Is the hitter getting the proper backside rotation?* (Refer to Figure 7-1, C-G.) Please keep in mind that correct backside rotation is "reactive"—not "proactive." It has been proven, anatomically, that it is impossible to "push" the hips (and lower body) open in the baseball swing. "Squishing the bug," a cue used by many coaches, is an "afterthought" in the swing, and incapable of the highly sought-after "hips-leading-hands" swing condition. In actuality, correct rotational hitting implies that the hips are initiated in the stride with the FRONT foot, relegating backside rotation to its correct reactive position in the swing. It is also *relative*, and not an absolute. Here's why: When the hitter swings at an outside pitch, he must make contact with the pitch deeper in his contact zone than if he had swung at a pitch that was inside. Because of this more rearward impact area and shorter length of stroke, the hips will normally have a reduced impact on the swing, as backside rotation is retarded. This is correct and natural. However, on pitches three-quarters in, the hitter must display good backside rotation, as his length of stroke (not to be confused with a "long" swing) increases. His back half is naturally pulled through by the sheer momentum of his rotating body. By so doing, the hitter will help optimize his bat speed and quickness to the ball.

❑ *Is the hitter's stride too long?* (Refer to Figure 7-1, A-B.) I'm not a big advocate of the long stride. In fact, the trend today is little or no stride. While the stride is necessary to get to the proper launch position (body BALANCED and on the toe of the lead foot), it is NOT necessary for power or bat quickness! It is basically a timing-and-"rhythm" movement that should also properly set up a hitter's axis of rotation. A long stride can add to a hitter's problems by creating timing inconsistencies. "Less is more" applies here!

An important point to keep in mind is this is a "style" issue! If possible, I RARELY change a player's style. HE has to feel comfortable and tension-free in his movements. Not ME. However, if he is not able to get to the PROPER launch position—ON TIME, then some adjustments must be made. The long stride can be one of the symptoms. If the player can't get to the proper launch position on time, he must play "catch up" with his other swing sequences. And, getting behind the "timing curve" has kept many from realizing their potentials by being late to impact.

❑ *Is the hitter getting "balanced" in the stride?* (Refer to Figure 7-1, A-B.) Not regaining the balance point in the stride will slow down and decrease the rotational velocity of the hips, producing less bat quickness and velocity. A good analogy is the spinning top. It will spin optimally for a long period of time, at its optimum rotational velocity, if it stays upright on its axis. However, as soon as the top begins to "yaw" (wobble), it quickly slows and falls down. By regaining the balance point in the stride (as opposed to holding too much weight on the backside and collapsing, or coming on to the front side and lunging), and being closely aligned with his axis of rotation, the hitter will optimize his rotational velocity, producing high bat speed and quickness and will help get him through the contact zone on time.

❑ *Does the hitter have a "plan" when he goes to the plate?* Managers in the major leagues get grey hair watching hitters, in favorable hitting counts—with men in scoring position—pop the ball up! If the hitter has been "studying" the pitcher that day, he should have a pretty good idea what to expect in a favorable count situation. In other words, *a smart hitter should never be late when the count is in his favor!* A good hitting plan helps the hitter be on time when it counts. Find out what your hitter is thinking. It could be he is way "off base" (no pun intended!) and can be corrected with some good advice and timely information!

❑ *Is the hitter doing the torque, numbers, and fence drills™?* I have my own proprietary drills, which I demonstrate on Tape #2 of my videotape set, "Do We Teach What We Really See?" These are the same drills I use to "de-learn" and "re-learn" rotational hitting. In addition to the instructional value, these same drills also act to keep the player "in the envelope" during his season. If a player is diligent doing his drills during the season, chances are, if he does run into a problem, it won't be a mechanical one. At that point, we can direct our attention to his thought process and his powers of concentration when he goes to the plate.

Summary Thoughts

I am sure you will find, as I have, that analyzing hitters is always a matter of subtraction, clarification, and the effective communication of timely, accurate information.

CHAPTER 8

"How Can I Improve My 'Two-Strike' Hitting?"

Many times, I have been asked to crystallize my thoughts concerning two-strike hitting. This factor has been an area of concern since baseball's earliest days. The ability to "put the ball in play," when hitters' backs are against the proverbial "wall," has tormented many players over the years and kept many individuals from hitting their potentials. This article, presents several ideas that are designed to bring both players and coaches to a better understanding of how to deal with this vital part of the hitting game.

This subject can really be simplified by understanding at the outset, that if a player stays "inside the ball," and employs good rotational mechanics, the only thing keeping him from becoming a good two-strike hitter is the mental approach he takes to the plate. First of all, to be a good two-strike hitter, a player has to "know" himself. I know, I know, I sound like a broken record on this point. But to deal effectively in situations where there might not be a "next" time, you've got to come to grips with "who" you are if you are to achieve your potential. You need to ask yourself several questions. What kind of hitter am I? Am I a better off-speed than fast ball hitter? Do I like the ball up or down in the strike zone? Do "like-handers" or "opposite-handers" give me the most trouble?

Second, to be a good two-strike hitter, a player must have a "plan" when he goes to the plate, and this plan is arrived at by knowing himself FIRST. He then gets his hitting plan from watching the pitcher, from his warm-ups before the first inning, to his most recent pitches to the previous batter. What pitch is he having trouble getting over? Is he an "against-the-count" pitcher? What pitch does he throw when he's behind in the count? Do I feel "comfortable" against this guy—or does he just have to "throw his hat on the mound" to get me out?

Answering these questions honestly can make the difference when the game is on the line, and it all starts with the opposing pitcher's first warm-up pitch. If you've done your homework, you have some choices. If you're facing a top-drawer pitcher who's making tough pitches that day, you may not want to "let" him get two strikes on you. Accordingly, you would expand your hitting zones and be more aggressive trying to put the ball in play, and not have to get to a two-strike count. If you feel there's no way that pitcher can get you out that day, you might want to shrink your strike zone somewhat and look for "your" pitch, knowing he "can't" strike you out.

When hitting against pitchers like Pedro Martinez, Randy Johnson, Kevin Brown, *et al*, very few—if any—hitters have a "dead red" area that day. Not surprisingly, few, if any, feel "comfortable" against pitchers of this caliber. But, everything in baseball is relative. In other words, even in *your* league, there are pitchers of this "caliber" relative to the others. So, in this instance, you probably won't elect to wait for "your" pitch—you'll probably never see it that day. Open up your hitting zones!

In other words, effective two-strike hitting involves knowing your strengths and weaknesses, who the pitcher is that day, and how "comfortable" he is to hit against. Doing your homework before each at-bat can add plenty of confidence and points to your OPS (on-base percentage + slugging percentage: baseball's benchmark for productive hitting).

As you read the articles in this compendium, you'll frequently see mention of how quickly at-bat situations can change. This factor, in turn, will affect your two-strike hitting approach. If you've got the potential to "go yard," and you represent the tying or winning run deep in the game, you may not want to make any concessions with two strikes. In a situation like this, there is no two-strike hitting. Your team needs the long ball from you. It's "outhouse or penthouse." Other times, and if you're not a "power" guy, contact, (i.e., "putting the ball in play)" is warranted. As a hitter, you've got to be aware of these factors and "hit according to your style."

How Does a Hitter Arrive at "Knowing" Himself?

All of a player's experiences playing baseball go into this equation. He is the sum total of every pitch, every at-bat, every inning he has ever played. Furthermore, over this time frame, he has learned what "type" hitter he is ("singles/contact hitters" for the smaller, fleet-of-foot player, "line-dive/gap hitters" who possess average-to-good foot speed and occasional power, and "pure power hitters" who tend not to run very well, but have true home run potential). Most hitters fit into these three types, and knowing where YOU fit in, goes a long way in determining your two-strike hitting plan. My experience suggests that approximately 70% of players fall into the "line drive/gap hitter" type, while the other two categories ("singles hitters" and "power hitters") have approximately 15% each.

"Cloning" Hitters

While we're on this subject of hitting "types," this is probably as good a time as any for all instructors/coaches to get on the same "page." Because most hitters fall into the aforementioned three types, you MUST be sensitive to the fact that not everyone can do what you teach. As an instructor, you have to adjust your knowledge of hitting—and what you teach—to the player and his intrinsic ability. Sadly, many times I tutor players who confide that their coach teaches everyone the "same" mechanics, regardless of size, strength, or foot speed. You must guard against allowing yourself to get caught up in this potentially harmful practice.

Last summer, a college player came to me for lessons. He was a big, strapping kid—6'4" and 240 pounds, strong as an ox. I asked him to take a few dry swings for me. After watching him, I told him I was really "excited." He asked why, and I told him that I very rarely come in contact with a player as strong as he was—and with such great foot speed. He looked at me, incredulously, and blurted that he had NO foot speed whatsoever. So, I asked him why he swings "down" at the ball if he can't run. He said that's what his coach taught, and EVERYONE had to hit the same way. Players 5'4" were taught to hit the same way as players 6'4"! At this point, you may be thinking "yeah, Mike, but that isn't ME. I don't do that."

Think again. Such a practice runs rampant in baseball. What a terrible waste of ability! His coach, possibly unaware of the consequences of his actions, was keeping this player from realizing his "dream." I told him I had no interest in teaching him mechanics that would upset his coach, and perhaps cast him in an unfavorable light in his eyes. He said he wasn't worried about that; his dream was to play professional baseball. Over the next two weeks, this player learned mechanics more suited to his "type." He returned to school and hit nine home runs in the fall. No one else on his team had more than two. At the conclusion of "fall ball," his coach came up to him and said he didn't like his swing. He wanted him to go back to swinging down—the mechanics he taught.

While this subject is being addressed, it is interesting to note, that as a "general" rule, ALL hitting types become "singles/contact hitters" with two strikes. Because, for the most part, you don't come to bat, every at-bat, where you represent the winning run. More often than not, you must do some things mechanically that will allow you to put the ball in play. The key point to remember is that contact—not power—normally becomes the name of the game with two strikes.

How Can We Gain More Time?

A large part of being a good two-strike hitter is the ability to "wait" as long as possible to determine what type of pitch it is, and where it is going. There are a number of ways a hitter can gain more time when confronted with a two-strike count. Over the years, many players have been taught to "choke up" on the bat, move further away from the plate, move deeper (further back) in the batters' box, and concentrate on hitting the ball up the middle, or the opposite way. Some individuals have been instructed to "close down" their stance somewhat, an action which offsets the hitter's contact points back further, and he gains him some extra time. All these suggestions have worked for many players over the years.

Another way, which I have found very effective, is for the player to move CLOSER to the plate, "open up" his stance, and utilize an inside-out swing (refer to Figure 8-1). By doing so, the player significantly shortens the path of his swing. His stroke is shorter (can get to the ball quicker), he rotates less, and he has more "accuracy," because he is more compact. My experience also suggests he will "open up" his hitting areas more effectively this way, rather than by closing down his stance. I also recommend this approach to all the "singles/contact hitters" I teach, because their greatest asset is their foot speed; the last thing they should want to do is jeopardize their contact-ability by increasing the length of their stroke.

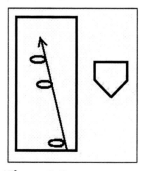

Figure 8-1

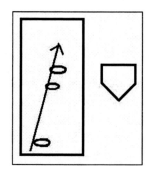

Figure 8-2

On the other hand, when a player closes down his stance (placing his lead foot closer to the plate than his rear foot, Figure 8-2), he effectively "closes off" to the pitch that is "in" and "down and in." With two-strike hitting, the idea is to "open up" your hitting zones, not close them down. And, by closing down in his stride, he not only runs out of hip rotation, resulting in an upper-body swing that loses bat quickness and bat speed, he also blocks off a significant part of his strike zone: the areas "in" and "down and in." In the major leagues, giving the pitcher an extra 25% of the plate to work with usually gets you a one-way ticket to a bus league.

The Inside-Out Stroke is Normally Used for Contact

Staying "inside the ball" is an integral part of hitting success. It makes no difference what "type" hitter you are, this concept works for EVERYONE. The article that I wrote on "Staying Inside The Ball," goes into much more comprehensive detail about its merits and why it should be on every hitter's "hit list." You are encouraged to (re)read it.

The inside-out stroke enables the hitter to wait longer. Coupled with proper lower-body rotation, the player is able to contact the ball deeper in his hitting zones. Harry Heilmann, the Hall of Fame outfielder for the Detroit Tigers in the '20s—who hit over .400 twice in his career—said he went from being a "good" hitter to a "great" hitter when he learned how to inside-out the fastball on the inside corner—when he had two strikes. This is a wonderful piece of information for all hitters. What he was telling us was that by being able to keep his bat 90° to the oncoming pitch on the inside corner, he was able to hit the ball back through the pitcher's box.

You can ONLY accomplish a proper inside-out swing by doing two things: 1) keeping your hands inside the ball, and 2) using good lower-body, rotational mechanics, whereby the hands have the ability to wrap around the rotating body as your arms extend toward the pitcher. This produces the correct inside-out swing. When a hitter is able to do this, he picks up more TIME—the elusive and valuable commodity a hitter never seems to have enough of. And, with two strikes, he doesn't have to be as "conscious" of the inside fastball—he can wait longer—which then makes hitting the off-speed and breaking pitches much easier. It worked in Heilmann's day—and it's still working today with baseball's current crop of outstanding hitters.

A player who quickly comes to mind when I think of the inside-out stroke is Edgar Martinez of the Seattle Mariners. He puts on a clinic when he hits. If you get a chance to see him on TV, or are lucky enough to see him perform at the ballpark, watch closely

and you'll see what I mean. In reality, there are too many others to mention here. All you have to know is if players are getting all the headlines—and making all the money—they're usually the best examples.

Executing the inside-out stroke correctly will enable the hitter to get to the pitch more quickly. He will not have to shorten his stroke. Again, it is worth noting that all

Photo credit: Christopher Ruppel/Allsport

hitting types should become singles/contact hitters with two strikes. The hitter has got to "give in" to the pitcher by shortening his stroke and gaining valuable time. I continually tell hitters that when they have two strikes, they can't anticipate pitches or "guess" with the pitcher. They can't afford to make a mistake here. They've got to concede to the pitcher and just put the ball in play.

Let's face it. With two strikes, the fight for time becomes amplified. The hitter is now dealing with his "largest" strike zone and also is confronted with the loss of the benefits of "anticipation" as an aid.

Proper Thinking

In two-strike hitting situations, "proper" thinking helps the hitter to get to all his hitting zones and "time" every pitch. The hitter has to prepare himself for every speed pitch in the pitcher's arsenal that day. That's why it is a good idea to see as many pitches as possible from that pitcher (make the pitcher pitch!). The best way to do this is to mentally prepare for the "in-between" velocities of the pitcher you're facing. In other words, if the pitcher has three pitches—one 70 mph, one 80 mph, and one 90 mph, the hitter must prepare for the mid-speed (80 mph) pitch. If he only has two, say an 85-mph fast ball and a 75-mph slider, you'd gear up your pre-swing for the 80-mph velocity.

As a result, the hitter gives himself a "chance" to catch up to the faster-speed pitch, yet still be able to stay back and put the off-speed pitch in play. Gearing up for one of the extreme velocities would put the hitter at a grave disadvantage: too late on fast balls and too early on off speed pitches. With two strikes, "proper" thinking prevails.

Ted Williams once told me that when the slider became popular, around 1950, that it was the hardest pitch for him to hit. So, he would "lay" for that pitch on every pitch.

From his earliest days, he felt no pitcher could throw a fast ball by him. I didn't fall into that category (and neither do the majority of major league hitters). Having ability like that will reduce anyone's strike-out potential, but the point to be made here is that he prepared for the mid-velocity pitch on nearly every pitch. By using the mid-velocity pitch as a timing benchmark, a hitter "should" still be able get to a slightly faster or slower pitch. However, the prevailing thinking is to look for the fast ball and react to the off-speed pitch, until you have two strikes.

Reaching Potential Demands Good Two-Strike Execution

To me, the quality of a hitter's technique lies in the superiority of his two-strike execution. By executing efficiently, he will bring a new-found confidence to his game. Once Harry Heilmann learned how to inside-out the two strike fast ball on the inside corner, and hit it back through the "box," he KNEW there wasn't a pitcher alive who could throw a fast ball by him. Likewise, when Ted Williams realized that he could "look" for the slider (mid-speed pitch) and STILL hit the cheese, he knew he was "on" to something. Statistics bore of these individuals. ANYTIME a hitter can "forget about" a pitcher's fast ball, the confidence this brings him is overwhelming. This is what we call being "comfortable" at the plate against certain pitchers. Being "comfortable" leads to "confidence," and having "confidence" with two strikes is the name of the game for the hitter. The fast ball "sets up" EVERY pitch in a pitcher's repertoire. And when a hitter doesn't have to worry about the fast ball—because he can catch up to it even when he isn't "looking" for it, he should rarely be fooled. As a result, the hitter can "sit" on his pitch, and be more selective—even with two strikes!

Hitters with little (or no) confidence normally fear getting to two-strike situations, and almost always open up their hitting zones prematurely to guard against it. The rule of thumb is when a hitter is ahead in the count, his strike zone should shrink; he can look for a "certain" pitch. When he is behind in the count, his strike zone should expand; he can't be selective. The hitter with poor two-strike execution invariably lacks the confidence to get to two strikes. In essence, he is "always" hitting when he is behind in the count. Few individuals have had success hitting this way. These hitters will swing at borderline pitches, because they lack the self-confidence to hit effectively with two-strikes. And by so doing, their batting averages and overall production radically tail off. Reaching potential demands first-rate, two-strike execution.

Don't "Sell Out" to Two-Strike Hitting!

On a number of occasions, I have seen players have success with their two-strike hitting approach and slowly gravitate towards adopting this hitting "style" on a full-time basis. The player should not be tempted to do this, nor should the coach/instructor persuade the player to do so. In my opinion, there is little more distasteful in baseball than seeing a player who can really drive balls, short-circuit his potential by adopting a singles/contact approach at the plate with less than two strikes. They should leave singles hitting to the bona fide singles hitters. The point to always remember is that if you've got serious "pop" in your bat, keep working hard at being the run producer you're capable of being!

CHAPTER 9

"Just How Important is Bat Speed?"

Bat speed is VERY important, but it is dwarfed in importance by rotational mechanics, as I will show later in this Chapter. If you want to hit the ball hard, you've got to have bat speed to do it.

Where Does Bat Speed Come From? How Do We Get It?

When we can harness the physical movements it takes to maximize bat speed, then we know that the bat speed we have is "optimum" for the physical resources that we individually possess as a hitter. Perhaps, some history can help us glean a clearer picture of bat speed and our obsession with it over the past generation.

I personally feel that there has been an overemphasis on bat speed since the advent of the aluminum bat in the early 1970s. With the introduction of the ultra-light, minus 12 aluminum bats in the 1970s, players could—and did—substantially increase their bat speeds. After all, we're talking about physically mature players swinging 20-22 ounce bats. Coupled with the super-high resiliency factor of aluminum, players were able to effectuate exit-speed ball velocities of well over 100 miles per hour!

In 1993, I read a report that stated that the "average" major league bat speed was 78 mph. I've heard many other "average" speeds over the years, including Mark McGwire's 91 mph in 1998. However, I'm not sure there really is a "norm," because different instruments and methods of calculation and quantification can yield varying velocities. While bat speed is important, I believe that individuals may be way "off base" championing it as THE universally sought-after commodity.

What *is* particularly striking to me—as a hitting instructor—is the detrimental effect that the quest for maximum bat speed has had on good hitting mechanics. With an ultra-light -12 bat, a hitter could stand at the plate and hit "clothes-line" line drives and hit balls well over 400'—by simply "flicking" his wrists. We became an instant era of hands/arms hitters—because we COULD be. The hitter's total body was no longer needed like it was before the arrival of the ultra-light aluminum bat. We could *drift*, and we could *lunge*, and we could get our weight on the front side and STILL be productive. The bat did all the work! We became automatons, more or less incidental to the physical swing process itself.

Biomechanics? Physics? Strength? Size? Balance? Not needed. Nearly everyone could hit the ball hard and become a power hitter. Many players were taught to "open up" their strike zones and were advised not to let too many "hittable" pitches go by, because when you had a cannon in your hands, don't waste it looking for a "good pitch to hit." If the pitches were around the strike zone, they were good enough to put a swing on. Batting average and home-run records in high schools and colleges were being reset on an annual basis. Sadly, we entered the "era of the twenty-second hitter."

While these ultra light aluminum bats benefited amateur players, those individuals who turned professional really got the "short end of the stick." Amateur players, transitioning from aluminum to wood bats, really struggled. The transition proved exceedingly difficult, because wood bats did not have the high resiliency factor of aluminum. The hitter himself had to do more. Much more. And do it correctly. The bat could not be relied on to do the bulk of the work. So, in an effort to lighten the bats to approximate the feel of aluminum, less-dense wood was used. Unfortunately, as wood bats became too light, the wood lacked the resiliency *and* density to drive the ball. Have you ever wondered why some wood bats have a "scalloped-out" barrel end? This was done to accommodate hitters used to swinging aluminum bats. It was done to lighten the bats. The bat manufacturers began using denser wood and then took a portion of the wood out of the barrel end, reducing the bat's weight, while attempting to maintain its density. It was the "only" way hitters could swing light bats and still get "decent" wood. Yet, we still continue to see a rash of broken and splintered bats interfering with hit balls in games where wood bats are used. It's become a "war zone" out there in the infield and on the pitcher's mound. When I played, it is difficult to remember a bat actually breaking in two separate pieces (or more).

And, I can't tell you how many good young hitters I have seen get signed to good bonus contracts, and, 2-3 years later, tell me they got released. "You're kidding me," I would say to them. "No, I'm not, Mike. I couldn't hit with a wood bat." Sure, they could have. But, they found that the productive wood bat swing required more than just a hands-and-arms approach. Mechanical changes were needed to offset the wood bat's increased weight and diminished resiliency.

With the introduction of the ultra-light and extraordinarily-resilient aluminum bats, players and coaches, alike, touted "bat speed" as the new "key" to productive hitting. But, over the years, as aluminum bats became heavier and the bat's resiliency was reduced to take players out of harm's way, bat speed also began to wane. In 2000, when the NCAA mandated -3 bats to be used exclusively, we saw hitting production and home runs decrease by 25%, a startling number. And, this trend is continuing. Many college coaches became accustomed to having four to five players hit double-digit home runs per year; now, they're seeing barely two players hitting this benchmark, the balance of the squad in the 0-5 home run neighborhood. Here in San Diego, hitting averages and production in high schools were down across the board. It should have signaled a "wake-up call" to coaches that changes and adjustments were in order. But, I don't think we've responded in a timely fashion and, in many cases, still continue teaching what we were taught when we played—which are the same mechanics when bats were -12s and -10s. The -3s are our "wake-up call;" it's time to respond.

I did a hitting seminar for a high school attended by 200 people last winter. When it was over, I had the pleasure to speak personally with many of the players and parents who attended. Some went up to the high school coaches, standing less than ten feet away from me, and thanked them for bringing me in to speak.

When most everyone had left, the head coach approached me and said that my talk was "really interesting," and "who can refute the videotaped swings of all the great players utilizing "torque" in their swings?" But, he said he would not change his hitting philosophy. "This is what I learned when I played. It's what I know. I'm not going to change." While I didn't say anything to him, my first thought was that this was not about HIM—or me—it was about his players hitting their potentials. I'll bet some of those players had D1 or professional aspirations and were counting on their coach to help them get there. Fortunately, all coaches certainly don't share this myopic attitude. Most coaches I know are very professional and continually search for ways to improve their hitters. As coaches, we need to be on the leading edge of what is being done today. We can't live in the past. We must take our egos out of the equation. We're no different than any others who are in positions of leadership—baseball or otherwise. We've got to make it a point to know what's going on. We've got responsibilities to those who believe we can help them attain their goals. OUR "work ethic" is just as important as our players' work ethics.

That incident notwithstanding, judging from my emails and the questions posed to me at seminars and on my website, we are beginning to come "up to speed" here. For a hitter to approximate the bat speed of a -5 (or lighter) with a -3, it takes much more than just a "hands-and-arms" approach. It requires the use of the hitter's entire body. The biggest and strongest muscles in our bodies, the legs, *must* be used to compensate for the heavier bat. This is the foundation for rotational hitting mechanics that are supplanting the linear hitting (back-to-front, hands and arms) which ruled during baseball's last generation. We know this change is going on because we now hear the same coaches that used to use the cue "come forward" now saying "stay back." The -3s have crippled the ultra-high bat speeds of days gone by. And while bat speed is important, it's just *part* of the story.

Does high bat speed mean that a player who can swing a bat 85+ mph is "guaranteed" power and a high batting average? Hardly! If a player can swing a wood bat upwards of 85 mph, and the bat is 35" and 35 ounces, then, yes, I would say that is terrific bat speed, and the player could be capable of outstanding power-hitting potential. But, what if the same player achieved that same bat speed swinging a 31"-28 oz. wood bat? Would he be able to hit the ball as far and as hard with a bat four inches *shorter* and seven ounces *lighter*? Probably not. Herein lies the paradox of the concept of "bat speed:" *Bat speed—in and of itself—can be a very poor indicator of power and hitting potential!*

When I played in the mid-1960s through the mid-1970s, nearly every major leaguer swung a 35" bat. Most weighed 32 ounces and up. Because of my relationship with Ted Williams, many ask what size bat he used. Ted swung a 35"-33 ounce bat. Personally, I swung a 35"-34 ounce bat. In contrast, Dick Allen, a terrific hitter of moderate size when I played, swung a 36"-38 ounce bat. And before Williams' era, many players swung 36" bats. Some upwards of 40 ounces. Most were considerably smaller than today's players. No one lifted weights. It's interesting to note that up until a few years ago, 42 of the top 50 home run hitters in major league history weighed LESS than 190 lbs. Why—and how—could they do this? In pre-aluminum bat days, *it was all about rotational hitting and generating torque*. Today's generation of players came up swinging light aluminum bats with their hands and arms. But, this is changing, also. Because with the use of the TOTAL body, players can use slightly heavier and longer bats more effectively than before. And, this has helped change the complexion of major league baseball's offense.

In their effort to capitalize on bat speed due to the lightness and resiliency of the aluminum bat, the bat manufacturers were able to sacrifice the one "key" ingredient in the power recipe: MOMENTUM. Momentum is the product of the bat's velocity AND mass. But, the super high resiliency of aluminum rendered momentum practically useless. It wasn't needed.

Another prime consideration should have been the length of the lever (bat) the player was using. For example purposes, we know it is far easier to move an object with a long lever than a short one. Leverage is the key. If a bat is too short, the hitter loses the leverage required to assist his momentum. While it is true that it does take more physical *energy* to break inertia and move a longer lever than a shorter one, this movement can be greatly assisted by the torquing of the upper and lower bodies in the swing. Using just his hands and arms, the hitter would have much difficulty breaking his inertia with a longer, heavier bat, in the time frame normally conducive to success.

Momentum is what helps generate a player's power, and this includes *mass*, *velocity*, AND *leverage*. (For me, it is fascinating to note that as players became much BIGGER and much STRONGER during this aluminum bat period, the bats became disproportionately SHORTER and LIGHTER. One would logically think it would be just the opposite. We can learn something from this.)

OK then, I hope things are becoming a bit clearer. The SIZE of a player's bat is just as important as his bat speed. Yet, over the past 25 years we haven't had to pay much attention to this because of the high resiliency of the aluminum bats. But, as the aluminum bats ultimately devolved into -3s, and the metal's resiliency was diminished, we collectively wondered where our power went. To effectively compete with these new bats, adjustments must be made. Rotational mechanics imply that we use the biggest and most powerful muscles in our bodies, our legs, to help generate high bat speed. As players began to couple their bat speed with a larger mass to increase their momentum through the contact zone, power numbers have increased significantly over the past 5-6 years (in major league baseball). As more hitters begin to use rotational mechanics and incorporate good lower-body technique into their swings, the power and production will be there. I liken this to "effortless power versus powerless effort."

Please don't mistake what I am saying here. Bat speed IS important. Very important. But, only if the player's bat is the longest and heaviest he can personally use EFFECTIVELY. No "macho" stuff here; there's too much at stake! The bat has to be the perfect compromise for all the criteria mentioned earlier. It is astonishing how many bigger players (aren't they all these days?), 6'2" through 6'6"—who have come to me for instruction—who bring 33"-30 oz. bats with them. And, they tell me that that's the heaviest bat they can swing! Or, the players that should be swinging a 35" bat, but can't find one, because the aluminum bat manufacturers "currently" don't make them in that size. They shake their heads in disbelief at the end of my instruction program, because their bats feel like toothpicks. Are they any stronger when they finish with me? No. They're just able to swing a longer, heavier bat AT NEAR (OR EQUAL TO) the bat speed they could with their shorter, lighter bats. As a hitting instructor, this is singularly one of the greatest gifts I can convey. Nothing magical here. Rotational mechanics—coupled with the vital torque position—make this happen.

There's also another very important issue to think about. And it's not about bat speed, either. It's about bat "quickness," the time interval it takes between launching your swing and making contact. To me, bat quickness is more important than bat speed. Many refer to this as "quick hands," but in reality, what they see, is the lightning-quick response (tight "linkage") to the correct torquing of their upper and lower bodies. It's why I continually tell players/coaches/parents at the seminars/clinics I speak at, that "torque"—the separation of the upper and lower bodies—is the root of all bat speed, bat quickness, and power in the good, rotational baseball swing. THIS should be every coach's goal, not just bat speed. Maximizing a player's bat speed is a product of the correct torquing of the body. Quick hands and high bat speed are reactive to this kinetic link.

These biomechanical movements are for EVERY hitter, not just power hitters, because the whole idea is to hit the ball HARD. Power hitters will stay behind the axis more (to create a slight upslope, consistent with their hitting type) than line-drive "gap" hitters and singles/contact hitters, who need to incorporate a somewhat "flatter" plane to their swings.

Make no mistake here. If players want to hit the ball hard, they've got to have bat speed to do it. There are myriad players out there who already have a great head start with high bat speed. Just don't neglect bat size, momentum, leverage, and bat quickness, which should also be sought-after ingredients in the total-swing recipe.

CHAPTER 10

"I'm Confused by the Statement 'History is Made on the Inside Half of the Plate.' Can You Tell Me What This Means?"

I didn't understand this brilliant statement when I first heard it, either! It came up in one of my first hitting conversations with Ted Williams, when he became the manager of the Washington Senators in 1969. A problem many players have is they don't ask questions when they're not quite certain what their coach is telling them. The fear of asking a "dumb" question has kept many players from hitting their potential in this game. So, I naturally agreed with Williams—and heard it many times thereafter from him—but it wasn't until years later, that I *really* understood it, and it all began to make sense. Hopefully my explanation will not only make "sense" *to* you, but make "cents" *for* you, too!

In a recent newspaper article, for-sure Hall of Famer Tony Gwynn made some interesting comments during a conversation he had with Williams in 1992. Here are some excerpts from the article:

GWYNN: "Ted [Williams] changed my game. Ted really ragged on me. He looked at my 31-ounce bat and called it a toothpick. He thought a guy my size should be driving the ball more and using a bigger bat. It was the first time somebody like that had really gotten on me. And, I found I really liked it. Because, it wasn't like you were just hearing another tip from another player. It's like you were getting preached to by the bishop of a church.

"At first, it was more a matter of me being in awe of Ted Williams. But then, I started to absorb the things he was saying. For years I'd hit the ball to left [opposite field] and be satisfied. He showed me different."

WILLIAMS: "Son, major league history's made on the ball inside. You show them you can handle that ball, then they'll throw it out where you want it. They won't pitch you inside."

GWYNN: "*Handle* is hitting it out of the ball park. *Handle* is taking a guy's best heater on the inside and driving it down the (right-field) line, *hard*.

"I always had the kind of stroke where it was hard getting the barrel head out in front..., I had the kind of swing that was good *to* the ball, but not *through* the ball."

WRITER: "How very ironic...that when Gwynn finally began driving the ball the way Williams had suggested, he suddenly was the greatest threat to Williams' exalted status as the last .400 hitter. Not since then has Gwynn finished any season lower than .321.

No one has more admiration for Tony Gwynn and what he has accomplished in this game than I! As good a hitter as he was, he realized the significance of Williams' advice and understood its task in taking him to the next level. While Tony was fortunate to have a few hitting discussions with Ted, I've had too many to count. And every time, I would learn something new—or at least *finally* begin to understand where he was coming from.

Ted loves to intimidate people, and, at first, I proved no exception. He'd insult me, berate me, and tell me he was "wasting his time" mentoring me. He'd cuss at me, laugh at my ideas, and continually chide me by saying "for a smart guy you sure ask dumb questions!" But, once you know Ted, you know this is his *modus operandi*. Scant moments later, he would bellow "That's right! You're on to something there! Now, what if a hitter could ..." or "Do you think that ...." And, we'd be off on yet another tangent. You get the picture.

He was tough. *Very tough.* He reminded me of Sean Connery in *Finding Forrester*, a movie I really enjoyed because of the mentor-student relationship. Ted had his own inimitable way of challenging me to help take our conversations to the next level. Many times, he would put me on the brink of total frustration and intimidation and then suddenly stop short and—almost whispering—say something like, "Do you realize the things we're talking about here? *Nobody* talks about these things." The gentleness of his tone made me realize the respect he had for me and the sanctity of our level of discussion. It was then that I realized both the agony and the ecstasy of interacting with—and being mentored by—this thoroughly brilliant, unique, and dynamic man.

I have said countless times, being mentored by Ted Williams has given me insights into hitting afforded to very few. Thanks, skipper, for sharing your knowledge and experiences with me. And for keeping me challenged and focused throughout the years in the pursuit of simplifying the toughest thing to do in all of sports.

Over twenty years before he shared the same insight with Tony, Ted used to tell me, "History is made on the inside half of the plate." But, until a player learns the mechanics that will *allow* him to get to the inside pitch effectively, he will continue to get jammed and break bats, or be too early, roll his wrists, and hit a harmless ground ball to an on-side infielder. Getting to the inside pitch correctly, however, is worth the effort it takes to learn, because its pronounced effect on increased production is limited solely by the player's ability to master it.

In my videos, I have spoken often about the three core mechanics of 95% of baseball's Hall of Fame hitters: the *hips lead the hands, matching the plane of the swing to the plane of the pitch*, and *staying inside the ball*. All of them favorably impact the hitter's approach when fully effectuating Williams' magnificent statement.

❏ STEP #1: The hitter must be able to clear his hips and get his bat head through the ball.

To hit the inside pitch effectively, the hitter must learn how to correctly clear his hips BEFORE he launches his swing. In other words, *his hips must lead his hands*. He accomplishes this, in his stride, by "separating" his upper half from his lower half, creating a stretching of his abdominal (oblique) muscles. I call this the "torque

Photo credit: John Gichigi/Allsport

Sammy Sosa in the classic "torque" position.

position," where the upper body is going back, while the lower body is coming forward. By setting up this "rubber band" (slingshot) effect, his hands will be *yanked* forward, as his hips begin their violent forward rotation, thereby enabling the hitter to get his bat head through the strike zone with his hips already out of the way.

If the pitch is inside, the hitter *must* be able to clear his hips correctly—not by "spinning," which often winds up yielding a centripetal, or "outside-in" swing. He must correctly initiate his hips to "pop" a split-second before his hands are yanked forward by the tremendous rotational velocity of the biggest and strongest muscles in his body (legs). NOTHING can get the hitter's hands through the strike zone quicker than this biomechanically correct movement (i.e., the "kinetic link") of separating the player's upper and lower halves. Torquing is the linchpin for maximizing bat speed, bat quickness, and power in the good rotational swing. *The hands are reactive to these proactive movements of the lower body.* If the hitter wants to be able to hit "through" the ball, not just "to" the ball, as Gwynn did, this is where it all starts!

As more players today begin to rotate more effectively, they also begin to experience and feel these many benefits that accrue from it. Yet, there are many players still being taught to hit with a closed front side and being instructed to keep their front foot "closed." This will hinder the player from hitting *through* the ball and getting into the classic "power vee" position seen in these photos of Sammy Sosa and Rickey Henderson. If the player doesn't (can't) get to this position on the pitch middle-half in, his power and production will suffer. Ichiro Suzuki of the Seattle Mariners is a prime example. He is a terrific hitter, albeit a "hands-and-arms" hitter who thrives on pitches away—the "power vee" for these types of hitters (i.e., those with little or no lower-body rotation). Tony Gwynn was a similar hitter.

Photo credit: Jonathan Kirn/Allsport

Photo credit: John Gichigi/Allsport

Ichiro Suzuki in classic linear hitter's "power vee" position.

Photo credit: Stephen Dunn/Allsport

Sammy Sosa and Rickey Henderson in classic rotational hitter's "power vee" position.

The full extension of these players comes somewhere in the vicinity of inside their front leg. They fight off the inside pitch. Both great hitters who have a different approach and technique—rotational for power and production and linear for singles/contact.

❑ **STEP #2: The hitter must "match the plane of his swing to the plane of the pitch."**

When a swing is launched, its initial plane is somewhat down. This *slight* downward plane continues until it is within 3"-5" *in front of the lead knee*, where it begins to level off. It stays basically level for a very *short period*, until it begins to pass the lead knee, where it begins its slight upslope. The slight upslope continues until the player has finished his follow-through. What we see is a swing that launches in the vicinity of the rear shoulder and terminates in the vicinity of the front shoulder. From the side—or "open" view of the hitter—during this ballistic movement, we see the classic shallow "U" as the hands go down slightly out of the launch position, level off for a short period, and then rise as the swing progresses toward the follow-through.

How far the hitter takes the initial downward plane of his swing often makes the difference between power and production or singles and contact. A "cue" that I use with hitters is "scoop sand with the top hand," which helps restrict an extended downward plane. Coaches must remember that the barrel of the bat is ALWAYS below the hands at contact, unless the player swings at a pitch at his armpits (or above). I still hear some coaches instructing players to "keep the barrel of the bat above the hands." If the hitter wants to hit in all four corners of the strike zone, he's got to let the barrel of the bat naturally follow the laws of physics and biomechanics and allow his eye-hand coordination to take over! The barrel of the bat will find the ball; the hands should return to approximately the same spot each time.

Larry Walker seen hitting a high pitch and a low pitch. Same player, different swing planes.

When a pitcher gets "burned" by a hitter, it is generally in two areas: "up" and "in." We read it in newspapers and hear it in interviews with pitchers all the time: "I got the pitch up" or "I didn't get it inside enough." These are "explosive" areas for pitchers. When a pitcher gets the ball up, and doesn't have that good heater, or didn't set the batter up correctly, all he's doing is giving the hitter the "elevation" he needs to hit the ball a long way. Hitters that are serious about getting to the next level must learn mechanics that allow them to "tilt" their bodies and "weathervane™" (or adjust) their lead elbows in response to pitch location. When pitches are up, the lead elbow works "down," and the hitter's body is more upright. On pitches that are down, the lead elbow works "up," and the body tilts back more.

The two pictures of Larry Walker tell the story graphically for us. Identical lower body torquing movements have preceded two different swing planes in response to two different pitch planes. One up, one down. When we know what to look for, we see it all the time! Being able to do this correctly brings my definition of the "perfect" swing into much better focus: The perfect swing is the adjustment you make to the pitch you get. Being able to make the instinctive on-the-fly adjustments to the incoming pitch is crucial to good performance and making history on the inside-half of the plate. This allows the hitter to stay on the pitch plane longer. To do this, his lead elbow works down somewhat on the high pitch (conversely, the lead elbow works up for pitches that are down). Even a "flat" (level) swing—on a pitch up—can produce a tape-measure bomb! The pitcher has given the hitter all he needs by throwing the ball up in the zone. However, the same flat swing on a pitch down in the zone will normally produce a ground ball.

Photo credit: Elsa Hasch/Allsport

Okay, Mike, but these are major league hitters you're discussing. They're "expected" to do this correctly. Is it possible to teach younger, less experienced players? Absolutely. I'm doing this every day. Check out the photo of the Little League player from this past year's World Series. Pretty good mechanics (adjusting to the pitch up) for a twelve-year old, wouldn't you say?

Where pitches are contacted can make a difference in their exit trajectories. Here's why. To hit pitches on the outer-half of the plate, the player *must* wait for the ball to get "deep." When he does this correctly, he contacts the pitch in the slightly downward plane of his swing. This imparts a lower trajectory to the pitches he hits. Conversely, to hit the pitch middle-half in, the player *must* hit the pitch out in front of his lead knee— or else he won't get his arms extended, and get jammed. The path of his swing in this vital area is slightly up. The player's hands *must* be able to *follow* his rotating body around the axis he originally set up in his stride.

This basically answers the question, "Why are pitchers taught to throw down and away?" To hit the pitch in this area, the player must wait and let the ball get deep in his contact zone. Contacting the ball deep with the pitch away has a couple of counter-productive movements. First, since the initial plane of the swing is down, the results are normally a disproportionate amount of ground balls. Second, the launch-to-contact phase of the swing occurs very quickly, yielding a swing too "short" to generate much bat speed, momentum, or power. As Williams would tell me, "There's no history in this area." That's why pitchers try to throw there.

The pitcher's *unvarying* focus is ground balls for this reason. Anytime he can get a hitter to swing down at a pitch going down (which ALL pitches do!), he makes his coach/manager very happy. If a pitcher can consistently throw pitches for strikes in this area, he's gonna be a star. Make no mistake about that.

The good rotational swing *picks up* momentum, as the body uncoils and continues on its journey to completion. Hitters would be "wise" to learn how to hit the ball out in front of their lead knee IF the location of the pitch warrants it.

❑ STEP #3: the hitter must be able to stay inside the ball.

As I write this on my laptop, I am sitting in front of the TV watching the A's-Yankees ALDS playoffs. I am constantly being reminded by Steve Lyons (the Fox color analyst) that these players are "good" because they know how to stay "inside the ball."

In the picture of Ken Griffey, Jr., he is seen hitting a pitch that was middle-half in. Junior is seen hitting the ball out in front of his lead knee, in the swing's upslope phase. If his lower body didn't rotate, his hands would not have been able to *work in front of*—and be supported by—his body at contact. We see the same centrifugal swing in the photo of Sammy Sosa hitting. Being able to do this well will insulate the hitter from hitting "around the ball," a major culprit in the "lack of power" syndrome. This is another key difference between rotational hitters and linear hitters, and why rotational hitters have consistently out-produced linear hitters. Linear hitters and players who do not use their lower bodies correctly fight this pitch off, much like Tony Gwynn's comment earlier in this compendium: "I had the kind of swing that was good to the ball, but not *through* the ball."

Photo credit: Otto Greule Jr./Allsport

Photo credit: Jonathan Daniel/Allsport

Ken Griffey, Jr. and Sammy Sosa "slotting" their back elbows correctly.

Now that we have seen how good core mechanics facilitate getting the player into advantaged hitting positions, it makes it much easier to analyze Ted's statement. Hitters should always have a choice as to the type of hitter they aspire to be. However, one thing is certain: a hitter must hit according to his own personal "type." My experience has been that, given the choice, every hitter wants to be "productive" and not a not a "punch and judy." To do this, he's got to correctly hit through the ball. Too often, we do not know how to give the player the ability to do so.

Quoting once again from the Gwynn newspaper article:

> WRITER: "Basically [hitting the ball on the swing's slight upslope] meant Gwynn would have to change what clearly was a successful approach to hitting. Through his now legendary amounts of workouts on hitting tees and film study, Gwynn had refined the most dependable swing in baseball, but he acknowledges he long had yearned for more pop. Williams gave him the impetus to find it in that toothpick.

Every player can be taught to do this. As coaches, we just need to have the experience knowing *what* to look for, and the knowledge *how* to teach it. If you do not have access to this information, it can be found in my videotape "Do We Teach What We Really See?" These same rotational mechanics have been used not only by Williams, but by 95% of baseball's Hall of Fame. If a great singles hitter like Tony Gwynn can say, "Ted [Williams] changed my game," why wouldn't we take a closer look at this time-proven hitting philosophy?

To "make history" in this game, the player has to be able to hit the inside pitch out in front of his front knee. In that area, the path of his swing is on the slight upslope and far enough along its journey to maximize his momentum and power. Good mechanics go a long way achieving these advantaged hitting positions.

CHAPTER 11

"Where Should I Stand in the Batter's Box?"

Where the player stands in the batter's box often gets little attention from coaches and players, yet it can dramatically impact his hitting success. Up in the box? Even with the plate? Back in the box? Close to the plate? Away from the plate? The relationships between the player's mechanics, the length of his bat, and the length of his arms all directly relate to the hitter's spatial proximity to the plate. And, all play into the hitter's predisposition for success or failure.

❑ *Hitter's ultimate goal*: *more time*. A hitter *should* always be looking for more "time" to look over a pitch. Delaying the ultimate decision whether a pitch is "worthy of a swing" is key to overall hitting success. Normally, the generally-accepted "standard" for a hitter's reaction time is approximately .40 second. In other words, a hitter has .40 second to decide whether or not to swing. Good friend and colleague, Dr. Tony Stellar, a true baseball "pioneer" in kinetic measurement, and the founder of Bio-Kinetics, tested this number extensively in his lab a number of years ago. However, he also found the AVERAGE major league "launch-to-contact" time-lapse to be .15 second. In other words, it takes the AVERAGE major league hitter .15 seconds just to get his bat from the launch position to impact, thereby reducing the player's precious decision-making time to .25 second—or less—depending on the efficiency of his mechanics, his personal "resources," and the plan he takes to the plate. It's no wonder hitting a baseball is the toughest thing to do in all of sports.

❑ *Up or back in the batter's box?* Notwithstanding this ultra-short reaction time, I see many players standing way up in the *front* of the batter's box! Some players who come for instruction tell me their coach told them that they could hit the breaking ball better if they hit it "before it breaks." I have no problem with this "cue"—provided it is not taken out of context. If the hitter is facing a breaking-ball pitcher that day who absolutely canNOT throw the fastball past him in ANY count situation—whether or not he is anticipating an off-speed pitch—then go ahead and move up. But, this should be the ONLY time. There are times, however, when the hitter will get some hits standing in the front of the box, and is subsequently lulled into believing that "moving up" was the reason. He then winds up staying too long with his new "good luck charm." He doesn't make the proper adjustments until the season is practically over, and extreme anxiety has already set in. Trust me, standing up in front of the batters box is tantamount to failure, and over the long haul, will ultimately reduce the hitter's chances for success. Hitters need time to be effective.

It's been a while now, but I think it was my good buddy, Dave Duncan, a former Oakland A's teammate who is now the St. Louis Cardinals' pitching coach, who told me an interesting story. It was in the early 1990s when he was the pitching coach for the Oakland A's. They were in Seattle to play the Mariners. Randy Johnson pitched against them and threw a two-hit (I think) shutout. Only one or two batted balls cleared the infield. He told me the A's hitters couldn't get around on his 100-mph fastball. During the course of the game, they made every hitting adjustment they could think of to quicken their reaction time. Nothing worked. After the game, "Dunc" went out and measured the "closing distance" between the pitcher and hitter. This number references the distance between the pitcher's *release* point and the hitter's *contact* point. What he discovered was the following: 1) many of the A's hitters were up in front of the plate trying to get to Johnson's hard slider before it broke. 2) RJ normally throws both his fastball and slider inside to right-handed hitters. To hit the inside fastball, the hitter must hit the ball out in FRONT of his lead knee (further decreasing the closing distance), or suffer the embarrassment of getting jammed and shattering his bat. 3) Couple all this with the length of Johnson's 6'10" long stride and his extraordinarily long arms, and well, you get the picture.

Taking all this into account, Dunc calculated that the closing distance was far from the 60'6" benchmark we routinely talk about; that day it was approximately 51 feet! Now, a hitter has only a fractional amount of time to make his go/no-go decision to swing. So, what the A's really saw that day were pitches coming at them at approximately 118-120 mph! This *further* reduced the .25 "normal" reaction time to around .21 seconds—almost half the universally-accepted .4 benchmark. No wonder he dominated and went through their lineup like a "hot knife through butter." The A's hitters increased the length of his fastball 3-5 "feet." *Why make the toughest thing to do in all of sports—tougher?*

❑ *In or away from the plate?* There is a direct correlation between the length of a player's arms, the length of his bat, and the distance he stands from the plate. Taking all these factors into consideration should be a primary consideration of every hitting instructor and player. Unfortunately, it is not. Ideally, the player should be positioned so that he gets good plate coverage on the low-outside pitch—without allowing his hands to go "to" the ball.

Younger players (perhaps 14 and below) have a much more difficult time covering the plate than more mature players. The younger players, with shorter arms and shorter bats, must still cover the same major league 17" wide plate (actually 20" when you factor in the plate's black outline). This is an almost impossible task, even with correct rotational mechanics, because their bats and arms are too short to cover the outside corner; they would have to stand on the inside corner of the plate to hit correctly. This is one of the principal reasons why players "lose" power when they get to be 13 and 14 years old. They've become so accustomed to "reaching" for the outside pitch, that they become "hands and arms" hitters, and continue to hit "around the ball."

To determine the correct distance, the player's arms should be measured from his armpit to the base of his palm. When I played, my arm length was 26". My bat length was 35". The optimal distance from the plate for me was about 13". Mature players will generally be in the 12"-13" range. This is for lower-body, rotational hitters ONLY, who can position themselves closer to the plate than can linear hitters. If the hitter "pre-extends" (bars) his lead arm in the approach phase, this will alter (increase) the east-west distance, as will "diving" into the ball. The goal for all hitters should be to keep the elbows "soft" and close to the body until extending through the ball.

By not reaching for the ball (left), the hitter is almost always in position to have his hands *supported* by his body at contact. An easy way to teach this is to have the player understand that hitting is like a pinball machine. Referring to the pinball illustration, one sees that the hitter must let the ball get deep when the pitch is outside. Conversely, with the inside pitch, he must get his bat head through the hitting zone much quicker. With the pinball machine, the bat is connected to an immovable station; it can't be moved TO the ball. The same goes for the hitter; his hands should not go "to" the ball! His hands should remain close to his body; they don't separate from his body until the arms begin their extension phase of the swing.

If a player keeps his hands correctly inside the ball, for example—Mark McGwire, he can situate himself considerably closer to the plate than the player who swings around the ball and can't keep his hands in close to his body during his swing. This is important, as it "takes away" the inside-half of the plate from the pitcher. Remember—that "history is made on the inside-half of the plate!"

I am continually reminded of a story I once read about Harry Heilmann, the Hall of Fame outfielder for the Detroit Tigers in the 1920s—who hit over .400 twice in his career. He said he went from being a "good" hitter to

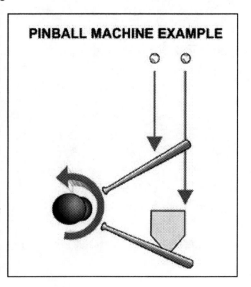

PINBALL MACHINE EXAMPLE

Barry Bonds in classic "approach" position. Any wonder why he is so great?

Photo credit: Otto Greule/Allsport

a "great" hitter when he learned how to hit the fastball on the *inside* corner right back at the pitcher—when Harry had two strikes on him. This is a wonderful piece of information for all hitters. What he was telling us was that by being able to keep his bat 90° to the oncoming pitch on the inside corner, he was able to "buy" time and hit the ball back through the pitcher.

We can ONLY do this by doing two things: 1) by keeping our hands inside the ball, and 2) by using good lower-body, rotational mechanics, whereby the hands have the ability to wrap around the rotating body as the arms extend toward the pitcher. This produces the classic inside-out swing. When a hitter is able to do this, he picks up more TIME, the elusive commodity hitters never seem to have enough of. Furthermore, he can stand closer to the plate where the "better" pitches are found. And, with two strikes, he doesn't have to be as "conscious" of the inside fastball—he can wait longer—which then makes hitting the off-speed and breaking pitches much easier. It worked in Heilmann's day—and it's still working today.

Rotational mechanics are for real. When we hit "around" the ball, the bat approaches the inside pitch more from the side than perpendicular, which severely limits the player from exposing the entire "sweet spot" of his bat to the oncoming pitch. And, he has to hit the pitch so far out in front (so he won't get jammed), that he loses the precious moments when he could be deciding whether it is even a good pitch to hit.

Okay, Mike, what did you mean there, when you said, "where the 'better' pitches are found?" Simply, hitters "see" pitches "close" to them better than those further away. They're easier to focus on, "track," and "target." When you see hitters far off the plate, often, the only way they can reach pitches outside is, you guessed it, by "reaching" and/or "diving" toward the plate. A hitter's spatial proximity is governed/restricted by the length of his arms and the length of his lever. Once he abuses this relationship, he can only reach for the ball away. This dramatically impacts the ball's exit-speed velocity, because it imparts an outside-in, hands-and-arms type swing.

In spring training, 1967, I was coming off a terrific Triple AAA season, where I was selected as both the *Sporting News* and *Topps* "Minor League Player-of-the-Year." I happened to be put into the same BP group as Frank Robinson, who was selected as the AL MVP the year before. Robby wasn't the easiest guy to approach, and when you're a "rookie," you're pretty much in awe of everyone and everything.

After watching me pull a few balls over the palm trees in right-center field, he came up to me and said, "You know, you can get better pitches to drive if you get closer to the plate, like I do." This made sense to me. I came up to the big leagues with a slightly closed stance, stood about 17 inches from the plate, and strode TOWARD it. Hey remember! I was getting advice from Frank Robinson here, a Hall-of Famer, and #4 on the all-time home run list! Why wouldn't I listen? So, I moved closer to the plate. And, in BP—against 60-mph fastballs—it really worked! I was crushing the ball. Big time. "Every" pitch was in my "red" zone.

We started playing exhibition games three days later. I played a lot the first week, as the club wanted to get a good look at me. Well, let me tell you, that week I broke an average of 2-3 bats per game. I got jammed so much, the "crotch" of my top hand stayed "black and blue" for the whole season. The reason I am telling you this story is NOT to make you smile (I know you did!), but so you or your players don't fall into the same "trap" as I did. Any time you change your distance from the plate (side-to-side), you MUST make corresponding adjustments to your mechanics. When I moved closer to the plate, I continued to stride closed (in, toward the plate). When I was back further off the plate, I could do this. When I moved closer, I was too "tied up" to get my bat-head through. Plus, it greatly magnified the fact that I wasn't staying inside the ball correctly. Even when I got my bat-head through, I couldn't keep the ball fair. I pulled them all foul, and always found myself hitting with two strikes.

Robby gave me good advice. I just wasn't smart enough to make the adjustments needed, until two years later, when I hit 30 home runs for Washington. But, I wasted two precious years! My purpose for writing these articles is to reduce this learning curve through good information. Been there, done that. So, the moral of the story is don't "be like Mike." Ask questions when someone gives you "advice"—even "Hall of Famers." You'll find that many of your great hitters could DO it, but most do not understand HOW they did it. While advice is normally well-intentioned, make sure you have the mechanics to implement it. And make sure when you move side-to-side in the batter's box that you make the adjustments necessary to complement your own "personal resources." What works for someone else, might not be appropriate for your talent/ability level.

I guess some players can do it, but I couldn't. I mean I could do it, but I couldn't DO it. When you see a pitcher like Tom Glavine, who lives on the outside corner, you're tempted to move closer to the plate, hoping to "bring" the pitch closer to your red zone. Any time—and every time—I did this, I "lost" my personal, "memorized" strike zone. When I attempted this, I wound up swinging at pitches TOO FAR outside, because that was my "memorized" strike zone. I actually wound up helping pitchers who threw like that. As my mentor, Ted Williams, used to say, "Dumb. Dumb. Dumb."

I remember moving up closer to the plate when Mel Stottlemyre of the Yankees was pitching. He had that good sinker—especially in Yankee Stadium with the short right-field porch. He only wanted to "eyewash" me with a pitch inside. Outside was where he wanted to get me—and other power-hitting left-handers out. But, I know I helped him get me out by moving closer to the plate. In my opinion, the best remedy for this type of pitcher is to have a plan when you go to the plate, STAY PUT, and exercise some plate discipline. Then, let the pitch get "deep" and take it the other way. It'll work wonders for you. And, yes, I wish I knew all this when I was playing …

Is There a "Perfect" Spot?

In an ideal world, the location of the "perfect spot" is where the individual player can cover all four corners of the strike zone and still put a good swing on the baseball. Okay, but where is it?

When I first started documenting my research, I said that to teach hitting we must simplify mechanics to the point where they are understandable to both the coach and the player. Forget about the player's "style," and concentrate on his "technique," and cut out all the superfluous gibberish that keep players scratching their heads—and restrains them from hitting their potentials. This also applies to "positioning" in the batter's box.

"Where" the player stands is a by-product of his mechanics and his personal resources. Pure and simple. And once an individual understands this, a common thread becomes readily discernible: linear (back-to-front) hitters are generally further from the plate than are rotational hitters. Researching this factor over many years, I have found the ideal spot for most rotational hitters is where they can make contact with the majority of pitches just out IN FRONT of the plate. After the player strides, his 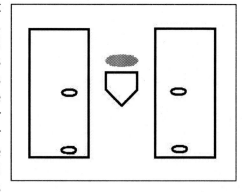 stride foot will come within a few inches of the front edge of the plate. Hitting the pitch middle-half in should be no problem, as the player can make contact slightly out in front of his lead knee, right in front of the plate.

Where he is supposed to hit that pitch. On the pitch down the middle or middle-half away, the player will let the ball get deeper, and take the pitch back through the middle, or to the opposite field, depending on pitch and contact location. I have shaded this area in the diagram, so that it may be more readily seen. In order for the player to be able to hit in this advantaged location, I have also found that his positioning in the batter's box is critical. The player's front (stride) foot should be abeam the plate, where the plate begins to "angle back" at a 45° angle. His distance to/from the plate may change as he physically matures and/or the length of his bat changes. I think what is reassuring at this point is the fact that the player does not need to keep experimenting north and south or east and west in the batter's box every time he runs into a funk. Lessening the variables in hitting—i.e., *simplifying*—is a real key.

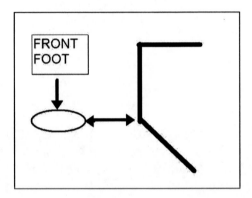

At best, especially in amateur baseball, the batters box isn't always chalked "correctly." Sometimes, the player *can't* line his stride foot up correctly with the plate, because the batter's box is too "short." In other words, his back foot would be out of the batter's box. Smart hitters cure this early-on by "wiping" out the chalk line in the rear of the batter's box. You'll see this in major league games all the time. Look for it. By the second/third inning, the chalk line has magically "disappeared," allowing the hitters to more easily position themselves advantageously. It's another of the little "edges" the hitter looks for that can make a big difference that day. Urge your players to take "swipes" at the back line in their first at-bat. If the player lines his front foot up with the plate as shown in the diagram, he will never be too far back in the batter's box. Being too deep in the box can mean "losing" the front-outside corner of the plate from a breaking ball like-handed pitcher.

This should all be pretty basic. Regrettably, most of this is done on a "trial-and-error" basis by most hitters. If a hitter is continually being jammed, rather than determining what his problem may be MECHANICALLY, he'll find himself drifting further from the plate. Then, he'll wind up reaching for the pitches middle-half away. I think this is one of the reasons we see players in so many radical locations in the batter's box. And, personally, I also believe this is another reason why we have so many people espousing different "hitting styles." This causes confusion. Correct the illness-technique, not the stylistic symptom!

CHAPTER 12

"Will I Lose Power If I 'Open Up' Too Early?"

Hitters often hear the statement, "you'll lose power if you 'open up' too early." This information has been heralded by most coaches over the past 30 years, and has resulted in many hitters believing that being "closed" and "square" to the ball is the only "ideal" body position. But, is it?

In the past, the aluminum bat, with its ultra-high resiliency and inherent ability to free the player from being "jammed," may have given some merit to the concept of being "closed" and staying "square" to the ball. The hitter could stay closed, get jammed on an inside pitch, and still hit the ball hard. The entire aluminum bat was a "sweet spot!" Unfortunately, for today's hitters, the new minus 3s have put a severe "crimp" in the works. The minus 3s no longer have the superlative characteristics of years past, including being light weight and having ultra-high resiliency, which they did when they were minus 7s and minus 5s. Minus 3s are too close to having the same "feel" and characteristics as wood, and hitters are now finding out the difficulty overcoming the increased weight with a hands-and-arms approach. They must make adjustments, because, in addition to the increased weight, the aluminum bats are now less forgiving and make it more difficult for the hitter to "fight off" the inside pitch. As a result, the bat can no longer do all the work; the dependence now is on the body's mechanical efficiency. If the technique is not there, it can make for a very LONG offensive season, filled with a lot of SHORT hits.

"Wind the Rubber Band!"

"Winding the rubber band" is an easy cue to teach, and much more descriptive than the biomechanical term for this action—the "kinetic link." Pitchers and hitters should both "wind the rubber band." But, while pitchers are taught this movement naturally, hitters are not. Far from it. Every pitcher is taught to open their lead foot completely in the stride. By completely, I mean they are taught to point their foot directly at home plate. Why are pitchers taught to do this? Because, it allows the hips to open. And, this action, coupled with the counter-rotating upper torso, creates "torque," which is the root of all speed and quickness in athletic movement. As the "linkage" between the upper and lower torsos "tightens," the forward momentum of the largest musclemass in the pitcher's body (legs) "yank" the smaller muscles (hands and arms) toward the plate.

Kevin Brown in the classic "torque position."

Consider Kevin Brown. His mechanics reflect the classic "torque" position (separation of the upper and lower torsos) utilized by all pitchers—open lower-half, closed top-half. "Winding the rubber band" is the key for pitchers, and SHOULD be for hitters. But, it isn't, because today's generation of hitting coaches are former players who were taught with the ultra-light aluminum bats. They naturally teach what they know best, i.e., linear hitting, which is primarily a hands-and-arms approach and a "closed" front side. As a result, hitters get very little, or no, benefit from their powerful legs.

So, why is it "right" for pitchers, and not "right" for hitters? I honestly don't know. But, either nobody sees it, or if it is seen, nobody can *teach* it. Although he clearly recognized early-on its critical importance in the productive baseball swing, my mentor, Ted Williams, never thought it was "teachable" either (until I developed and demonstrated my proprietary hitting drills to him. These drills reduce the emulation phase from years to days, through progressive instruction). Nonethetheless, it has been passed on through *emulation—not through instruction*—at the major league level for 100 years. In fact, 95% of baseball's Hall of Fame hitters have utilized this concept and have reaped its many benefits. However, while the big leaguers all do it, they don't know they do it, and they can't tell you *how*. Go figure.

As in pitching, there is NO reason a hitter will lose power if he opens his front foot in the stride. In fact, he will GAIN more power if he counter-rotates correctly! However, the hitter *must* let the pitch get "deep," stay inside the ball, and *counter-rotate his upper torso* to make it all happen.

Let's try to simplify this. You've heard me mention on several occasions to think of hitting as a pinball machine. In a pinball game, because the bat is mounted on an *immovable* post, we are unable to move the bat to the on-coming pinball to hit in varying locations. As a result, we must "time" the oncoming pinball correctly. To hit an oncoming pinball that is "away," we MUST let it get deep, or we "run out of bat." We can't reach it, or we'll hit it off the end. If we move our hands "to" the ball, which is away, essentially we're casting—hitting around the ball. Getting our hands into an "unsupported" position like this does absolutely nothing for balance, bat quickness, or power. Conversely, if we perceive the pinball to be "inside," we MUST meet it out in front; we've got to get our bat head through the zone. We can't let it get deep, or we won't get our arms extended, and we get jammed. *The arc of the pinball-bat swing doesn't change; hitters just make contact at different points in that swing-arc.* If we lock-in our lower halves, we greatly amplify the problem. Hitters must have the mechanics to deal with pitches in these varying locations. If we don't get our hips open in the stride and "wind the rubber band," we're essentially giving this advantaged hitting zone back to the pitcher. Doing so has ruined many careers and restrained many talented players from hitting their potentials.

When pitchers make "mistakes," they are usually in two areas: "up" and "in." Hitters have to "rake" in these areas. You know, I can't remember hearing a pitcher say he gave up a three-run homer on a tough, low-outside pitch. As hitters, we hit pitchers' *mistakes.* Make no mistake about that. Good pitchers are good because they make fewer mistakes than the average. A hitter won't last long if he doesn't have the mechanics to "rake" in these areas where the mistakes are made.

The hitter cannot "give away" the *inside half* of the plate by *always* being "away-conscious." If a hitter is always looking away, dives into the pitch, locks his hips, or keeps his front side closed when he strides, do you honestly think he'll be able to get his bat head through on an inside pitch? Williams used to tell me and my Washington Senators teammates that "history is made on the inside-half of the plate." Hitters have to have the mechanics to be able to pounce on pitches middle-half in. If we lock in our hips or our front side by striding with a closed stride foot, we're severely limiting our ability to work effectively in the advantaged inside-half zone; *we're blocked out.*

How Is This Done?

However, I would be the first to agree that if a player opens his lower half early in the stride WITHOUT counter-rotating his upper torso and keeping his hands back, he's in for trouble. Big trouble. He's got nothing left. But, with correct rotational mechanics, the player is taught to "wind the rubber band," counter-rotating (closing) his upper-half, while simultaneously opening his lower-half. As the player's stride foot turns out, his lower-half then opens. This allows the hips to come through and lead the hands to the ball. Without opening the stride foot, the hips would lock in, thereby preventing correct lower-body rotational movement, which restricts bat speed, bat quickness, and power. For example, compare Ken Griffey Jr. to Kevin Brown.

Ken Griffey, Jr., in classic "torque position."

Photo credit: todd Warshaw/Allsport

To effectuate this action correctly, there are certain "core" mechanical movements that must be followed, with each player's personal "style" wrapping around these core mechanical movements. It is the reason hitters *look* different to us. But, the universal core movements are there nonetheless, and easily observable, as shown in my videotape set, "Do We Teach What We Really See?" They are *universal* and do NOT change.

For the most part, linear hitters are 1) closed front-side, 2) closed-stride, and 3) front-foot hitters (weight going to the inside of the *front* thigh). On the other hand, rotational hitters 1) *open* the stride foot, 2) hips lead the hands, and 3) the weight goes to the inside of the *back* thigh. Over the years, linear hitters have been primarily singles/contact hitters, while rotational hitters have been the run producers and power hitters. The "opening" of the lower half—early—coupled with the torque position, has made this possible. "Effortless power versus powerless effort" aptly describes the difference.

Can We Measure "Torque Angle?"

All hitters have a certain amount of "stretch" between their upper and lower halves. Short and wide players have less stretch than tall and thin players. It's just a fact of life. When you see a tall, lean player, like a Ken Griffey, Jr., you see a hitter with more abdominal "stretch" than the average player. In fact, Griffey Jr.'s "torque angle" is 40°—greater than any other player in the major leagues.

The extent to which a player is able to counter-rotate is dictated by the amount the player opens his front foot in the stride. Theoretically, if the player strides fully closed, i.e., 90° (or more) to the plate, he should be able to close his top half more than if he opened his stride foot at a 45° (or more) angle. Each player has to be considered uniquely, in order to optimize each individuals personal "assets." As coaches, we should be vigilant to never allow a hitter to be able to turn back so far that it impedes his focusing on the pitch with BOTH eyes. To do this, keep in mind the relationship between the player's own ability to stretch, how "open" his front foot is in the stride, and how far he can counter-rotate before "losing" the advantage of his rear eye. A hitter will lose his depth perception without having the use of *both* eyes.

Another important factor to consider is you really don't want the player to already be fully "closed on top" in his stance. Sure, Griffey, Jr. does, but he does it because he CAN—his neck appears to be double-jointed! The average player would find this very restraining, if not impossible. Because as your top half is counter-rotating, your lower half is also opening—*at the same time*. And, before the upper half gets *completely* closed, the player's front heel will drop, initiating hip rotation. The explosive force of his hips, firing forward, will yank his upper half to the ball BEFORE his hands get completely back. This "fly-rod" or "rubber-band" effect is why we see elite players appear to have such fluent swings and display "effortless" power. It's all working correctly for them.

The key point to remember is that the universal technique (mechanics) is identical, regardless of where the pitch location is. However, if a hitter "takes his hands with him" in his stride—*even if he strides closed*, he most definitely will not have "anything" left. Remember that "winding the rubber band" is the key in this instance. Teach or learn the mechanics involved in how to do this CORRECTLY and reap the benefits.

CHAPTER 13

"What Approach Should I Take When Hitting in Various Contact Locations?"

Far too many coaches and players make hitting much more complicated than necessary. On the other hand, others make it far too simple.

As easy and straightforward as I try to make it, the cue "see the ball—hit the ball" is TOO simple and fails to meet my personal tutoring expectations for two valid reasons. One of these failings is that it implies that the hitter must not "move" until he sees the ball leave the pitcher's hand. I can assure you, that if a hitter does this, he'll almost always be "late." A hitter must break inertia long before he "sees" the pitch. In effect, he "dances" with the pitcher. Second, as I will point out later in this article, hitters concede too much to the pitcher by taking this approach, because it implies looking for *every* pitch in *every* contact location, which is a very tough proposition for any hitter.

The first step to keeping it simple is mastering the technique of baseball's elite hitters: the *hips lead the hands, matching the plane of the swing to the plane of the pitch, and staying inside the ball*. These moves are "universal" and have been used by 95% of baseball's Hall of Fame hitters. EVERYTHING else in hitting involves personal "style." I always advise coaches and players to master the technique FIRST; it will take the confusion out of instruction. Once learned, the player's "personal" style will seamlessly wrap around the "universal" technique. *Naturally*. And, when a player runs into his inevitable funks, a coach can help him immeasurably by correcting—what legendary University of Hawaii coach Coop DeRenne used to say—his "illness-technique" and not his "stylistic-symptom." This simplification process works wonders getting the player untracked.

Cover One Side of the Plate Until You Have Two Strikes.

Again, the idea is to simplify, not confuse. For a hitter to hit in various contact locations, he must remember one cardinal rule: *a hitter can only cover ONE side of the plate*

EFFECTIVELY on any given pitch. Period. When hitters try to do too much, they usually wind up doing very little. In other words, "less is more." To illustrate this point, many coaches teach hitters to "use the whole field." There's absolutely nothing wrong with this cue—except when the hitter tries to do it on each and every pitch. Then, he winds up trying to hit on—or cover—both corners of the plate on every pitch, which is an extremely difficult thing to do. Essentially, *the player is hitting with two strikes all the time,* because the only time a hitter should be protecting *both* sides of the plate is when his proverbial back is to the dugout. He's forced to—he has two strikes and can't afford to take a close pitch. By "using the whole field," hitters must hit the inside pitch out in front of the plate, and, conversely, to hit the outside pitch, they've got to let it get "deep." This strains ability to the *nth* degree, because the difference can be as much as five feet from one contact area to the other! Timing BOTH of these pitches presents a physical challenge for any hitter.

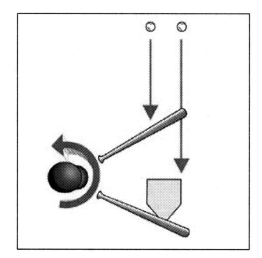

Anticipation

Until a batter has two strikes on him, he *should* be in the "driver's seat." He should look for his pitch and/or location. By that, I mean he should be "anticipating" pitches. So, let's define "anticipation" first. To me, it is not "guessing," because that implies taking a "stab" at something: maybe—maybe not. Anticipation means making a decision based on *known* facts. HOW has the pitcher been pitching me? In or out? Up or down? Fastballs or off-speed? Is he an against-the-count pitcher? Once the hitter has a "book" based on actual information, he is on his way to gaining the "head start" he needs.

Thinking along with the pitcher is a fascinating science, and can greatly simplify hitting in different contact locations. The quality of information he's gathered constitutes his "plan" when he goes to the plate. I'm convinced that the truly great hitters in baseball have been able to "slow down" the game, not only through ability and mechanics, but by an uncanny ability to *mentally* store up information. Having this information handy helps take the element of "surprise" away from the pitcher and improves timing. And by so doing, they greatly increase the size of their "dead-red" area—while simultaneously shrinking the "size" of the plate they have to cover!

You should now see that I agree that hitters SHOULD use the whole field, but only by *anticipating* pitches with *less than two strikes*. LOOK for the pitch in an anticipated area—and if you get it—put a good swing on it. *All* hitters should see a huge increase in their power and production numbers utilizing this basic approach.

A simple example in this instance would be a pitcher who "can't" work inside, so the bulk of his pitches are away. Up until two strikes, the hitter should be anticipating a pitch away. I know this about hitting: if I'm looking for a pitch in a specific area, and I get it, I should be able to hit it. Ask any hitter: "Do you think you will be late if you're only looking for an inside fast ball?" Every hitter will tell you that, *if they're looking for it*, they shouldn't be late. Same goes for a specific pitch. "Do you think you could hit a change up if it is the only pitch you are looking for?" Same answer again. We DO hit—and most times hit HARD—what we *look* for!

Hitters normally aren't fooled by a curveball's spin or trajectory. Really, it's just depth perception, hand/eye coordination, and balance. Hitters are fooled by the *change of speeds*. So, if a hitter is anticipating a curve ball, and gears up for its speed *only*, he'll stay in a "balanced" position longer, keeping his weight from coming forward, and lunging. *The timing of the stride goes hand-in-hand with the amount of weight the hitter offsets in his approach, and both are determined by his anticipation.* Why do pitchers continually change speeds? To keep the hitter off-balance. Hitters need to counteract the pitchers' mission by destroying the pitcher's plan. It is done through anticipation and taking away the element of surprise. This greatly levels the playing field for the hitter in his confrontation with the pitcher.

However, I don't understand what it is with today's hitters. Maybe it's a "macho" thing, because it makes absolutely no sense to me. Ask today's hitter if he "guesses," and he'll tell you "no way." No? If the count is 2-0, and the only pitch the pitcher can get over for a strike is a fastball, what would YOU be looking for? We ALL guess (whether we want to admit it or not), but today's hitters have the impression it's not "macho;" it's for "sissies." Baloney. ANYTIME THE HITTER CAN TAKE THE ELEMENT OF "SURPRISE" AWAY FROM THE PITCHER, HIS PRODUCTION GOES UP GEOMETRICALLY. *Surprise* (changing speeds and locations) is the pitcher's greatest weapon. Take it away from him, and the hitter's chances for having fun get much better.

Timing is More Important Than Location.

So, why do so many hitters have so many problems? Everyone knows hitting's a tough thing to do. But, hitters make it tougher by not taking the time to formulate a plan when they go to the plate. And, they pay dearly for this indifference. In the big leagues, most hitters only want to know "location:" inside or outside. Most don't care *what* type pitch it is—only *where* it is! Why? Because, they have more time with the pitch away, than with the pitch in. It's all about "timing." A hitter can hit in ANY location if he times the pitch correctly. Even if the hitter is looking outside, and gets his pitch in that area, he still won't hit it if he doesn't time it correctly. *Timing is more important than location.* I say this to major league hitters, and they look confused. "I never thought about it like that, Mike." Well, *when potential is at stake, a hitter's got to know!* The earlier a hitter learns this, the better off he'll be.

And, how do we get over this timing "speed bump?"—by anticipating pitches based on a known set of factors: WHAT pitch is the pitcher getting over for strikes and WHERE does he want to pitch me. Once the hitter crystallizes this in his mind, he can start formulating his plan. Until the pitcher has two strikes on him—when he's FORCED to cover both sides of the plate, he's in control. In short, the pitcher's got to "give in" to the hitter. If and when the pitcher does get two strikes on him, the hitter's got to give in to the pitcher, and protect both sides of the plate. But, this makes hitting much tougher, and will take the hitter's aggressiveness away. Now, the hitter's got to gear up for EVERY pitch in the pitcher's arsenal, as well as EVERY pitch location. Believe me, this is physically restraining for even the elite hitter. Historically low batting statistics with two strikes prove how difficult it is to cover both sides of the plate. Why make the toughest thing to do in all of sports *tougher*?

Body Positioning

"Timing" is integrally coupled with "body positioning." When players without "plans" are taught to continually look away to protect the outside half of the plate, they set themselves up for not being able to "pull the trigger" on the pitch middle-half in. They'll consistently get jammed, or take the pitch by "jackknifing" away from it. The same holds true for the hitter who always looks for the pitch inside. He will continually "pull off" the pitch middle-half away and be early. *By anticipating a pitch correctly, a hitter adjusts his body to cover the part of the strike zone where he is expecting the pitch to come.* If hitters are repeatedly told to look away, one of the pitcher's "mistake" locations disappears: the pitch middle-half in. However, if the hitter is "looking" for the pitch middle-half in because of "proper" thinking (good plan), he should have no trouble getting his bat head through the zone due to good body positioning and improved timing.

I realize most pitches are thrown toward the outside corner. They're thrown there for a reason. There is less chance of getting "hurt" in that area with a long ball. And, if the player is facing a pitcher that day who is consistently throwing strikes and hitting the outside corner, he has to adjust his plan accordingly by slowing down his pre-swing movements. He simply says to himself, "I've got to let the ball get deeper" and take the pitch the other way. If a pitcher can't get the ball down, or is a hard thrower who uses a four-seam fastball that rides "up," the smart hitter tells himself, "I've got to get my hands on top of the ball more." And looks for that specific pitch ONLY—up to two strikes. Briefly, a simple plan and anticipation can work wonders. And, equally important, good (hitting) coaches will advise their players of these patterns as they develop during the ball game, so they can help give their hitters that sought-after 51% edge.

The Technique is the First Step

Good hitting mechanics (technique) should be the starting point for every player. Because, even if the hitter anticipates correctly, but doesn't have the good mechanics to hit effectively in the area he is looking in, he still is not going to put a good swing on the ball. I have players coming to me for instruction all the time that tell me they get jammed—even when they're *looking* for the fastball. This shouldn't happen, and is normally a function of poor body positioning, due to faulty mechanics. That's why a blueprint for hitting potential should always begin with good mechanics. Proper mechanics allow the hitter to hit effectively (or as effectively as his personal resources will allow) in all four corners of the strike zone, but this happens infrequently.

Most hitters want "quick fixes" to their hitting problems. Cues like "throw your hands at the ball," "turn on the ball," and "pop your hips" rarely help a hitter if a coach doesn't show him how to do it correctly. He has to learn suitable mechanics, because THERE AREN'T ANY QUICK FIXES! It starts with some ability, a goal, a good work ethic, and good rotational mechanics, and all this then blends in with a smart hitting approach. My mentor, Ted Williams, always felt it was 50% from the neck up. I'll always remember back in 1972, when I played first base for the Oakland A's, and we were vying for the AL Western Division title. We were playing a wonderful Detroit Tiger team, in Detroit, late in the season, which we met in the AL playoffs a short time later. We were ahead, 2-1, in the bottom of the 7th inning, a runner on first base, with two out. Hall-of-Famer Catfish Hunter was on the mound. Up comes Hall-of-Famer, Al Kaline.

Tiger Stadium was a real band box, and Kaline had 399 career home runs. He was the last person we wanted to see hitting. Fifty Thousand people were standing and cheering their hometown hero. The count quickly went to 2-0. I think everyone on the A's held their collective breath as Cat threw the next pitch, a fastball right "down Broadway" for a called strike. My first thought was "whew!" We really dodged a bullet there. Kaline then took ANOTHER fastball right down the pipe for strike two. I couldn't believe it. Cat then walked him on two close pitches. Dick Williams, our manager, went out to talk to Hunter. I looked at Kaline, standing on first base, and said, "Al, how could you take those two fastballs?" He said, matter-of-factly, that he wasn't "looking" for them. In the shower, after the game, I asked Catfish if he was surprised Kaline took those "predictable" fastballs. He said, also matter-of-factly, that he couldn't remember ever throwing Kaline fastballs when Al was ahead in the count. He counted on him looking for an off-speed pitch! But, this example would also be appropriate if it was pitch *location*, instead of pitch *type*. Al Kaline did his homework. So did Catfish Hunter. The great ones do. It's like "counting cards" in Blackjack or Hearts. Players are great for reasons we many times never see. They've got their heads in the game. We coaches and hitters have to, also. The payback is in "spades."

To sum up, hitting in certain contact locations boils down to good mechanics *and* a good hitting plan. Used wisely, they'll take any hitter to the next level. If the hitter is anticipating a pitch away, he should automatically slow his pre-swing movements down a bit, so as to let the ball get a little deeper in his hitting zone. If he is anticipating a pitch in, he must quicken up a bit and *correctly* clear his hips. If he knows the pitcher wants to throw him upstairs, he should think about getting on top of the ball a little more, flattening out his lead elbow somewhat, and being a little more upright on his axis. If he is anticipating a pitch down, he needs to think about working his lead elbow up more, sitting down on his back leg, and coming back more on his axis. The operative word is ANTICIPATE. Everything should flow smoothly from this verbal "cue." Use it wisely and reap the results.

CHAPTER 14

"Clone the Hitter's Technique— Not His Style"

Given the many variations in players' body sizes and abilities, it is surprising that so many hitters look so similar. Tall players, short players, thin, stocky, strong, weak, fast, and slow. They're ALL different and easily distinguishable. To be sure, *emulation* plays a significant role in a player's learning curve. Yet somehow, over the past thirty years, the individuality of the hitter has been misplaced. Today, most hitters look "cloned."

What does *cloning* mean? The dictionary defines it as "to make multiple identical copies." For baseball purposes, the definition for hitters should be obvious. Unfortunately, I do not think this has been good for the hitter. In fact, I feel it has restrained many players from reaching their potentials and has led to as many players leaving baseball's ranks prematurely as any other single factor.

Timely Advice for Coaches

As I begin discussing hitting "types," this is probably as good a time as any for us instructors/coaches to get on the same "page," when it comes to classifying hitters. Since hitters fall into three distinct types, we MUST be sensitive to the fact that every hitter cannot do what we teach. As instructors, we have to adjust our hitting knowledge—and *what* we teach—to the individual player—his hitting *type*, and intrinsic ability. Players should not have to conform to the only thing we know how to teach. Sadly, many times I tutor players who confide that their coach teaches everyone the "same" mechanics, regardless of ability, size, strength, or foot speed. We must guard against allowing ourselves to get caught up in this potentially harmful practice.

Hitting "Types"

Two summers ago, an out-of-state college player came to me for lessons. He was a big, strapping kid—6'4" and 240 pounds. Strong as an ox. I asked him to take a few dry swings for me. After watching him, I told him I was really "excited." He asked why, and I told him I very rarely come in contact with a player as strong as he—*and with such great foot speed*. He looked at me, incredulously, and blurted that he had NO foot speed whatsoever. So, I asked him why he swings "down" at the ball if he can't run. He said that's what his coach taught, and EVERYONE had to hit the same way. Players 5'4" were taught to hit the same way as players 6'4"!

I know you're smiling at this point and saying, "Yeah, Mike, but that isn't ME. I don't do that." Think again. It runs rampant in baseball, and potentially short-circuits promising careers. As I looked at this player, I thought, "What a terrible waste of ability!" His coach, possibly unaware of the consequences of his actions, was keeping this player from realizing his "dream." I told him I had no interest in teaching him mechanics that would upset his coach, and perhaps cast him in an unfavorable light in his eyes. He said he wasn't worried about that; his dream was to play professional baseball. Over the next seven days, this player learned mechanics more suited to his type. He returned to school and hit nine home runs in the fall. No one else on his team had more than two. At the conclusion of "fall ball," his coach came up to him and said he didn't like his swing. He wanted him to go back to swinging down—employing the mechanics he taught.

Next season, because he didn't do as asked, he played in only nineteen games, despite leading the team with eight home runs. He wasn't drafted, but is one of the "lucky" ones. He has since hooked on with an Independent League team in pursuit of his big-league dream. What a shame that this kid became involved with a coach who espoused this type of hitting philosophy. I'll bet if he would have known this *before* he took his scholarship, he would have gone elsewhere.

Hitters Must Hit According to Their Types

Asking a big, burly kid with no foot speed to hit ground balls is asking him to fail. Accordingly, trying to make a frail, speed-burner type into a fly-ball slugger is equally cruel. What I find with many players I am fortunate to work with is that they all look the same. It seems few coaches have taken into account the variances in players' hitting types.

Classifying Hitters

I classify hitters into three distinct types: 1) the singles/contact hitter, 2) the line-drive gap hitter, and 2) the pure power hitter. All hitters fall into one of these three groups.

❑ *The singles/contact hitter*. The primary goal of the singles/contact hitter should be line drives and ground balls. These players normally have excellent foot speed and can take advantage of the ground ball. Usually, because they have little or no power, hitting the ball in the air doesn't make much sense. To take advantage of his unique abilities, he *must flatten* out his swing more than the other types of hitters. He should shoot for 50% line drives and 50% ground balls. To do this, he must sit more upright on his axis, resulting in a flatter swing plane than his counterparts. (Unfortunately, I see far too many hitters who have been made into singles/contact hitters despite their ability to do much more. Ability is a heartbreaking thing to waste.)

❑ *The line-drive gap hitter.* The goal of the line drive-gap hitter is to "balance out" the trajectories of balls off his bat. He normally has "average"-to-"good" foot speed and should hit for high total bases. He may have some power. He should shoot for 50% line drives, 25% fly balls, and 25% ground balls. His position on the axis is slightly behind center, facilitating a slightly steeper swing plane than the singles/contact hitter. Two distinct examples of this identical hitting type would be former Rockies' teammates Larry Walker and Jeff Cirillo. Both would be classified as line-drive/gap hitters. Walker has "plus" power and hits 35+ home runs per year, while Cirillo hits a ton of doubles. Both are the same type hitter, although Walker has a bit more power. As a result, he sits behind the axis somewhat more than Cirillo, so each gets different results. And both are terrific hitters!

❑ *The pure power hitter.* The last type of hitter is the pure power hitter. He has great power and size, but little, if any, foot speed. His goal is 50% line drives and 50% fly balls. Lacking any foot speed, ground balls to him result in too many outs. His position on the axis will be even further back than the line-drive gap hitter, because he needs to get the ball in the air more often to be effective.

So, while *each hitter should demonstrate the identical core mechanics,* their position on the axis normally determines what TYPE of hitter they are (or will become). The choice SHOULD be there for every hitter, but unfortunately, through cloning, it is not. Many times, we only turn out hitters who swing down and do one thing: hit ground balls. Ground balls are not the only "name" of the hitting game. While they may be for the singles/contact hitter, they certainly aren't for ALL hitting types. And, every hitter MUST hit according to his type! Where the hitter positions himself on the axis plays a large part in helping the player hit his potential. Moreover, each type of hitting not only has its own relative importance to the success of the individual player, but also to the team's collective offense.

While we're on this subject, it is interesting to note, that as a "general" rule, ALL hitting types become singles/contact-type hitters with two strikes. *Contact—not power— becomes the goal with two strikes.*

We should now be at the common understanding that the defining characteristic of each hitter's type boils down to where he *sits* on his axis of rotation. As you will see, the mechanics are identical for all three types.

Okay, now that we have a better understanding of hitting *types*, we need to look once again at the difference between the hitter's *style* and *technique*. We must know and understand this difference.

Many times, we hear hitting coaches talking about a certain player's "hitting style." I used to, also. But the more I thought about it, the more obscure this term became. A few years ago, I was speaking with a major league hitting coach during batting practice. He told me how "difficult" it was to stay current with the swings of each individual player. He said he had to know everyone's "hitting styles" perfectly, so he could make corrections if anyone went into a funk. As I listened, I thought to myself, "this person must be a genius. How could anyone "memorize" all the subtleties and nuances of every swing of every player on his team?" Talk about confusing!

Players DO NOT have their own, individual *hitting* styles. They have their own, individual personal styles, which ultimately couple with a *universal* hitting technique. They are as distinct and separate as cats and dogs.

Style

Style is "personal." Style is the individual player. All players have their own style. Style is determined on an individual basis by that particular player, based on a plethora of individual resources. No one but the hitter himself can determine what feels best for him. So, when we try to alter a hitter's style (e.g., "hold your hands high"), as instructors, we are doing him a disservice. We may be asking him to do "something" he is not physically capable of— or is uncomfortable with—at that PARTICULAR time.

A hitter's style is a result of his own personal "comfort" level; his tension-free way of relaxing based on "who" he is. All physical movements made by the player, prior to arriving at the launch position, is a product of his inimitable style. These moves must be comfortable and efficient for HIM. Personally, I NEVER change a hitter's style, unless he demonstrates that he cannot get to the proper launch position *on time*. Who better to dictate *comfort* than the hitter himself?

Technique

Technique, on the other hand, is not personal. It is "universal." One of the most intriguing phases of my development as a hitting instructor was being able to identify the identical movements being made by baseball's elite hitters, from the launch to contact positions. I have since called this phenomenon "being in the envelope." In fact, 95% of baseball's Hall of Fame hitters fit into this technique envelope! I call the movements within this envelope the *core mechanics*. Surprisingly, there are only three that I have been able to isolate: the *hips lead the hands, the ability to match the plane of the swing to the plane of the pitch, and staying inside the ball*. What could be simpler?

Clone the Technique—Not the Style!

If I have been effective breaking down the difference between style and technique for you, then it should easily flow to the next conclusion: "cloning" a hitter's style makes little sense, because every hitter is different. However, for a player to hit his potential, it can be effectively argued that getting a player to exhibit the same vital core movements of baseball's elite hitters does indeed make sense!

The progression is a normal one. After learning the core mechanics, the player's own personal style will "wrap around" the universal technique in his own "natural" way—for him and him alone. What works for one hitter might not work for another. When I teach, I use my proprietary drills to put the players in the advantaged hitting positions of these Hall of Famers. When they are done, they exhibit the core mechanics of baseball's elite, productive hitters: they are "compact" and "short to the ball." As they continue on and gain more experience, they incorporate their own natural style. They begin to "understand" what their bodies can and cannot do to be effective—based on their own, personal resources. Being able to make these adjustments is crucial to a player getting to the next level. The core mechanics, however, *must* remain intact. Assuming the hitter's technique does indeed stay "in the envelope," any subsequent adjustments made to the swing are normally style adjustments.

The Lineup

As coaches, we always seem to know where to hit certain players in our lineups, because we easily recognize the difference in hitting types. We normally hit our singles/contact hitters 1-2 and 7-8-9. Our line drive gap and pure power hitters we hit 3-4-5-6. Common sense, no? Why is this so easy for us to see, yet we tutor hitters to be all the same? Every player makes his offensive contribution, based on his hitting type and position in the lineup. A *balanced* lineup should be every coach's goal. Don't make 'em all the same and reap the benefits of an improved offense.

CHAPTER 15

"The Importance of Matching the Planes"

I know of NO coach who would send a pitcher out to the mound to pitch a ball game with only ONE pitch. Common sense (and experience) would tell you that by the second or third inning, the kid you ran out there would have had his cap "spun" so many times that he'd be ducking for cover. With only one pitch, the element of "surprise" the pitcher holds over the hitter quickly evaporates.

Yet, day in and day out, *incredulously*, many coaches routinely send up hitters to the plate with only ONE swing! If a player is taught to swing level—or down—at EVERY pitch, what chance for success does he have against a sinkerball pitcher, or one who can consistently keep the ball down?

Who's to Blame?

Recently, I attended a college game in southern California. It was a tie game going into the bottom of the ninth inning. The lead-off man lined a triple to the gap. Man on third, nobody out. The third base coach (the team's head coach) kept urging his batters to "Get the ball in the air! Get this run in! C'mon! Just a fly ball here." The opposing coach brought in a sinkerball reliever to try to get the hitters to keep the ball on the ground. He did his job well; no pitch was higher than slightly above the knees. Every hitter hit a routine ground ball. Inning over. Runner stranded. The opposing team scored in the top of the tenth and went on to win. The coach of the losing team was furious with his hitters.

JUST a fly ball? When we teach mechanics that make it difficult to get the ball in the air, who are we to blame? Our hitters? Our job as coaches is to put players into positions to succeed, not fail. But, when we march hitters up to the plate with only "one" swing, that is exactly what we are inadvertently doing. We wouldn't send our pitchers to the mound with only one pitch, yet we *routinely* send hitters to the plate with only one swing. Subsequent, we lament our lack of offense—or blame our hitters. Hitting a baseball is TOUGH enough and is not for everyone. Why make such a difficult thing to do even TOUGHER?

The Downward Plane

All pitchers, at some point, are taught to throw in a "downward plane." Many are tall, throw off a 10" mound, release the ball at ear level, and aim for the hitter's knees. Coupled with the effect of gravity and the fact that all thrown pitches "tilt" (break the plane), then only a person with "selective vision" would have difficulty seeing this natural phenomenon. If pitchers can get hitters to hit the sinking pitch on the ground, they've done their jobs well. No three-run home runs on those puppies! *Ground balls are a pitcher's best friend.* I recently read where 80% of the balls hit on the ground in the major leagues are outs. Why, then, do we teach hitters to HIT ground balls? If pitchers are "taught" to THROW ground balls, why do we accommodate them? I was listening to a coach a while back who was talking to his pitchers about the merits of THROWING ground balls. "That's your job," he told them. Twenty minutes later, he walked over to his "position players" and worked with them on HITTING ground balls. Does this make sense? Is it logical? It seems we all-too-often parrot information without taking the time to think it through.

Hitters Must "Tilt" to Avoid the "Tilt."

Based on your good feedback, it appears we're getting smarter. MUCH smarter. We're finally starting to question things. Do we really want hitters to be swinging "down" at pitches going "down?" When we "match the plane of the swing to the plane of the pitch," we're able to counteract and thwart the primary goal of the pitchers. Whatever pitchers do, the hitters have to adjust and do the opposite. I explain it by simply saying, *hitters must "tilt" to avoid the "tilt."* Put another way, the hitter must counteract the tilt of the pitch by tilting his body rearward, so he can initially get on the plane of the pitch. This is what smart hitting is all about, and is a principal reason why baseball's elite hitters manage to hit their POTENTIAL—and also why so many others never realize their lifelong dream.

In an effort to increase offense in 1969, major league baseball lowered the mound from 15" to 10". Up until that time, many major league pitchers were "over-the-top," fastball-curve, four-seam types. Throwing overhand indeed made sense, because the higher mound steepened the vital downward plane of the pitch. Anytime a pitcher can increase this downward plane, the more success he should theoretically have, because it makes it much more difficult for a hitter to match a steepened pitch gradient. In fact, one of the most difficult pitches to hit from overhand pitchers was the "12-to-6" curveball. The steepened gradient of the pitch entitled hitters to only ONE "swipe" at the intersecting planes of the ball and bat. Hitters never see that pitch anymore. Moving to the 10″ mound helped usher the overhand pitchers out of baseball. Look for them to start making a comeback now that the umpires are calling the high pitch.

When major league baseball lowered the mound, they ushered in the second great "offensive era" in baseball. Batting averages and production dramatically increased; it was now much easier for the batter to "match the plane of the swing to the plane of the pitch." It took some years before pitchers made their adjustments to the flatter mound. But, in reality, it's never been the same for the pitchers. Making these adjustments popularized a "new" pitching type: the "sinker-slider" pitcher. In an attempt to regain maximum downhill planes, pitching coaches had two directions to go: 1) find sinker-slider, two-seam pitchers who could impart more "tilt" (sink) to pitches; and/or 2) find and use taller pitchers.

Both options would have a similar effect because pitchers could recover a portion of the downward plane of pitches lost due to the lowering of the mound. As many of you are aware, major league scouting seeks out pitchers who are 6′3″ and up for this very reason. However, my personal feeling is that if baseball REALLY wanted to level the playing field for pitchers, they would raise the mound back to 15″. This move would be much less subjective and arbitrary than the route they have recently taken (increasing the size of the north-south strike zone). However, make no mistake here: for the pitcher, it's all about "tilt" and steepening the pitch's downward plane!

Mike's "Perfect Swing"

I hope you can now understand why my definition of the *perfect swing* is "the adjustment the hitter makes to the pitch he gets." *A hitter must have the mechanics that will allow him to do this*. We're not talking about a golf swing here—the ball is not sitting stationary on a tee, just waiting for us to smack it. The reality for hitters is that the ball is *moving through varying planes* on its quick trip to the plate. Just as no pitcher wants to throw at the same speed or to the same location on every pitch, neither does he want to throw "flat" pitches, or pitches that "flatten out." Doing so is tantamount to disaster for him and his team.

When speaking about pitchers and their strategies, we normally speak "east-west," as in inside-outside. But, as the player advances and plays against better competition, he will run into pitchers who also use "elevation" to their advantage. If the pitcher's kept the ball low for the first three or four pitches, AND HE'S GOT A COUPLE OF STRIKES ON YOU, he'll try a high strike. As hitters, we should know our eyes and mechanics can get stuck on elevation. Pitchers know this, too. Being able to "match the plane of the swing to the plane of the pitch" goes a long way in this instance in leveling the playing field.

Can it be that pitching instruction is so much further advanced than hitting instruction? Pitchers are taught to move the ball around. Up. Down. In. Out. In a hitter's perfect world, all pitchers would throw to the SAME location. In this perfect world, we could then get by with teaching only one swing. Unfortunately, a hitter's world is NOT perfect; we rarely get the same pitch thrown to the same location. And because of this imperfect world, we must be able to make adjustments to the varying locations and elevations of the pitches we get.

Pitch Location Determines a Hitter's Follow-Through

Many times, I am asked whether I advocate and teach a "high finish" to a player's swing. I tell them "no." Nor, do I teach a "low finish." With good rotational mechanics, the *location* of the pitch will determine whether the follow-through is high or low. Swinging at a low pitch should result in a higher follow-through than swinging at a high pitch, where the hitter flattens out his swing more to get on the pitch plane. Many players who come for lessons tell me that they have been taught to finish high ONLY—without regard for pitch location. I don't recommend this; swinging "up" at a high pitch is just as bad as swinging "down" at a low pitch.

Players who are taught to swing "level" on *every* pitch should ask themselves this question: *"Is it possible to swing 'level' at a pitch at my knees?"* If you're not sure, try it. And, if a player is only taught to swing "down," he is *forced*—through muscle memory—to repeat his swing that way on EVERY pitch. When players are in youth leagues, they can get by with this; youth-league pitchers have trouble with their control and many pitches are "up." They can hit this pitch with a "down" swing. But, as the player advances, and the pitching gets better, more and more pitches are thrown "down." If the player has only been taught to swing down at a pitch down, if he makes contact, he has little choice but to hit a ground ball.

A number of years ago, a major league hitting coach told me that most of the game's best hitters "dragged" their rear foot as they swung. He had a photo of each one to "prove" it. And, indeed, he showed me nine or ten pictures of some terrific hitters in this hitting position. Well, all these photos were players swinging at pitches at their shoulders! And, with this pitch location, they were executing perfectly—they were on the plane of the pitch! In other photos, I have seen these same players "sitting" on their rear leg and "tilting" to accommodate the steeper gradient of the low pitch. (When we study hitters, make it a point to look at numerous swings, encompassing different pitch locations and elevations, before making your evaluation.)

A hitter, swinging at a high pitch must "level off" his shoulders. By so doing, he will be PREDISPOSED to coming forward and possibly dragging his rear foot. Fact of life. Yet, I hear it all the time from coaches and parents: "Stay back—keep your shoulders level!" Sorry, guys, but this is physically restraining and confusing to the player; you've got his body going in opposite directions.

Occasionally, I get a player for my hitting program who cannot swing "up"—at all. I'll ask the player to simply throw a ball up and "hit it in the air." You would be surprised at how many individuals cannot perform this straightforward task; it has been ingrained into their mindset (that fly balls are "bad") and through drills (to swing down). "I can't. Nobody's taught me how" is the familiar refrain. A hitter must have many swings—all within the context of his core mechanics—to enable him to counteract the varying planes of pitches that he must face.

When speaking at baseball shows and seminars, I make it a point to tell my audience how grateful I am to the many unselfish players, coaches, and colleagues—past and present—who have contributed to my hitting education. In essence, that I am speaking to my audience "standing on their broad shoulders." My enduring task has been to crystallize this mountain of fact and fiction in a way that makes sense—and can be readily taught.

In addition, I tell them my only goal is to make them "think." Does the information I am presenting sound logical? Does it make sense? Are we teaching what we *really* see? If I can persuade the attendees—to simply ASK these questions, then I feel like I have succeeded—regardless what anyone does with the information. Because, ultimately, it will make us all collectively smarter—and better at what we do, which is winning games and helping our players hit their potentials.

As Gerry Spence, the noted trial lawyer, once said, *"I would rather have a mind opened by wonder than one closed by belief."*

CHAPTER 16

"The Importance of Correctly Positioning the Back Elbow"

"Stay inside the ball!" has become a popular coaching "cue" since the advent of the aluminum bat. To stay inside the ball, the hitter's hands must follow the rotating body around its axis. This is a difficult task to perform for linear hitters, who have been taught to keep their front side rigidly closed. As a result, the hitter's body is restrained from "rotating" around its axis. It is a back-to-front movement, not an angular one; the body doesn't *naturally* turn the corner like a rotational hitter. As a result, the hands don't either. The "locked in" front side prevents this from happening. Moreover, if the back elbow is up—and doesn't tuck in *close* to the player's body in the approach phase of the swing, the hands are *forced* away from the body as the rear elbow extends prematurely. Linear mechanics have produced a generation of players who hit "around the ball." It seems that every player I tutor must be corrected.

At seminars, clinics, and on my website, I field numerous requests by coaches and players alike, specifically seeking advice on keeping the hands inside the ball. It's a widespread problem.

It's Really Just a Matter of "Style"

If you have read the previous chapters, you know that a player's stance is part of his own personal "style." Because of this singular distinction, we must realize that a player's style, no matter how unorthodox or different it may appear from "normal," will be "right" for that particular hitter. If it's not, adjustments must be made if the player is to hit his potential. A player's personal style must flow efficiently and fluidly into the universal technique when his front-heel drops. As coaches, we must be smart enough to recognize this, because if we don't, the player can wind up contradicting the laws of correct biomechanical movement. Hopefully, you will see as we go on, that the "wrong" setup (style) can wreak havoc with a player's fluid transition to his technique, and ultimately, his performance.

What Does "Stay Inside the Ball" Really Mean?

"Stay inside the ball" is just one of the "cues" coaches use to restrain the hitter from letting his hands get away from his body during the swing. Among other coaches, the cues "knob (and/or hands) to the ball" and "hit the 'inside half' of the ball" are also common.

Let's review several factors for a second. We should know that high bat velocity is produced through the torquing (separation) of the upper and lower torsos ("kinetic link"), whose energy generation begins at the feet and is sequentially transferred up through the legs, hips, shoulders, arms, and hands. This energy INCREASES successively until it is maximized at the end of the bat, resulting in unparalleled angular velocity. What's important here is to understand that high bat velocity comes from these "linked" body segments.

The kinetic link works in conjunction with the hands staying inside the ball, which means the hands and bat remain close to the body during the sequential transfer of energy. For this to occur, the rear elbow MUST tuck in on the approach. The hand path stays circular, as the hips begin to decelerate, and the torso receives its maximum energy-transfer. "Extension" occurs as the swing nears the appropriate contact zone, which is normally dependent on pitch location.

The hands and bat travel in a circular movement as they follow the rotating upper body, with the barrel dropping below the hands on the approach to contact. The bat head will always be below the hands at contact—unless the player swings at a pitch above his letters, at which point the barrel of the bat could be higher than his hands as he attempts to get on the plane of the pitch.

Why is "Staying Inside the Ball" So Important?

Staying inside the ball (1) keeps the hitter "short" and compact, (2) maximizes bat quickness and bat velocity, (3) supports the hands at extension, and (4) gives the hitter more "time" to look pitches over. These features clearly show why it is one of the "core" mechanical movements I teach.

EVERY player whom I tutor has been "asked" to stay inside the ball. Every coach parrots this information; it's a very contemporary buzzword. But, while they ask the player to do this, many never explain it correctly, or teach other factors that make it practically *impossible* for the player to accomplish it.

For example, *combining* the cues "stay back" AND "swing with level shoulders" is a biomechanical impossibility, as are telling a player to "keep your rear elbow up" AND to "stay inside the ball." Both are equally frustrating and confusing. These cues not only *counteract* one another, but are restraining for even your elite athletes, much less those with lesser ability. Yet, coaches ask players to do this every day. Do *you*?

Many of these same players have been taught to keep their back arm/elbow up, and parallel to the ground. *Keeping the rear elbow up facilitates the down swing.* By so doing, the hitter's lead elbow *must* work down, resulting in a "level-shoulders" approach, a weight-shift forward to the front side, and a corresponding down-gradient to the swing. After all, we can't hit with *both* elbows up, can we? Or with both elbows down, either. A major consequence of this elevated rear elbow, linear-type swing is the predisposition to hit around the ball.

"Slot" the Elbow

No matter where the hitter places his rear elbow in his stance, it MUST "slot" (tuck in) at the launch position, for two reasons: (1) to allow the lead elbow to work up and help position the tilting body, so the plane of the swing can match the plane of the pitch; and (2) so the hitter can stay inside the ball. Both of these movements, coupled with the torque position, comprise the "universal" technique of 95% of baseball's Hall of Fame hitters.

A Ted Williams Recommendation

My mentor, Ted Williams, advocated "relaxed arms" in the stance. Having suffered through sub-par hitting seasons my first two years in the big leagues, when Ted became Washington's manager, he fixed my elbow-up, "long" swing, and "casting" problems. Can you see why the "book" on me was "hard stuff, in?" Pitchers at the major league level can consistently get it there. Good mechanics allow the hitter to hit in all four corners of the strike zone and help offset the pitching advantage.

Mike displaying his form in 1967. His inability to "slot" his rear elbow correctly on the swing approach led to two sub-par seasons.

Using this cue, and once having corrected my "hitting problems," I went on to enjoy one of the best years of my career (1969), hitting 30 home runs and winning the prestigious "Player Win-Average" award, given to the American League's "most productive hitter." (Willie McCovey won it in the National League that year). Years later, aluminum-bat hitting mechanics brought me to "grips" with the usefulness of Ted's advice. Sometimes, it's just a small tweak that makes a big difference; other times, a major makeover is in order. But, you've got to know WHAT to look for in order to correct the flaw. Then, you have to have the knowledge and experience to correct it!

Barry Bonds correctly "slotting" his rear elbow, producing an inside-the-ball swing.

Photo credit: Otto Greule/Allsport

"Picture-Perfect" Barry Bonds

Barry Bonds is a good example of a hitter who uses the rotational swing. His photo clearly shows why he is one of baseball's elite hitters. The swing pictured was his 69th home run (2001). The pitch was on the inside corner, yet he hit it to straightaway right field. He was able to keep the pitch fair because he stayed *inside the ball.* (Staying inside the ball allows a hitter to keep his bat as close to 90° to the oncoming pitch as possible.) Notice the position of his rear elbow, tight against his body. Working his rear elbow in this manner enabled him to elevate his front elbow, allowing him to get on the plane of the pitch. Also, notice the position of his rear shoulder. It must dip to stabilize the weight on the *inside* of his rear thigh (preventing him from lunging), and to allow him to match the pitch plane. WHY do we teach "don't dip the back shoulder?" *Do we teach what we really see?*

Emulation

Having the ability to "emulate" other hitters and their visible "styles" can be both a blessing and a curse. Many younger hitters have gotten into this casting mode by emulating major league hitters they see on television. While I am a big advocate of emulation as a teaching tool, it can also lead a hitter down an unforgiving path if it is not used with discretion. At times, we see some good major league players who hit with an elevated rear elbow. So, since they do it, it must be right. Right? In my experience, I find most amateur players who emulate these players tend to hit "around" the ball far more than those who maintain "soft" elbows throughout the swing, until extension. Many times, they are also "late" at contact. They're late because the barrel of their bat has to travel further to contact; the result of a longer swing.

Most big leaguers are able to make on-the-fly adjustments to pitches that many others cannot—especially on a consistent basis. Because they have the "resources" to do it; they're baseball's best!

Julio Franco's unique "style" has worked well for him.

No one in recent memory has the "style" (stance) that Julio Franco has, yet he is a terrific hitter. As you can see in the photo of Julio, the barrel of his bat is high over his head, pointing BACK at the pitcher! His own personal assets allow him to hit with this "style." The point to remember in this instance is that, when he launches his swing, he is able to "slot" his elbow close to his body. The core mechanics ("technique") he uses from that point on are identical to baseball's elite hitters.

But, if you were an instructor, would you teach your son/daughter or other budding players, to copy his style? Probably not. For every Franco, and those few that can do it, there are probably a jillion hitters we never heard of because they DID this very same thing—and got nowhere! The arm to watch, however, is the *rear* one: if it extends too quickly, the player is left with little choice but to hit around the ball. The back elbow must ultimately tuck in if we are to stay inside the ball!

Now, please don't misunderstand what I am saying here. I'm not saying one *shouldn't*—or *can't* hit—this way. A hitter has to be comfortable and tension-free. I tutor professional players down through younger players. And, while the pros invariably are more mature physically, more experienced, and have more advanced motor coordination (i.e., more resources), it puts many younger players at a distinct disadvantage.

A player *may* be able to "get by" doing this at the younger levels and in high school/college. But, as the pitchers get better and more competitive—and they use *both* sides of the plate more effectively, the hitter will have to make some compensating adjustments, or his "window of opportunity" closes quickly. The player MUST get to the universal launch position correctly—and on time, or he must be physically taught to do so. The earlier a player is taught correctly, the better off he'll be. It is the *rare* player who can control an elevated back elbow, have perfect timing, and stay inside the ball.

Cues

Some "cues" have hindered more than helped. Cues like "get your rear elbow up," "keep the barrel of the bat above the hands," and "chop down at the ball" do little for staying inside the ball. When a hitter performs these cues, he automatically raises his rear elbow, as his hands go upward and rearward.

And, how about the cue, "center the bat?" This cue puts the barrel-end of the bat angled back towards the pitcher, positioned over the button on the player's cap—and often-times beyond. This is accomplished in the pre-swing by "cocking" the bottom wrist and/or barring the lead arm.

Teachers of this cue "justify" it by saying it gives hitters a little more bat speed, and therefore, power. But, it also produces a "longer" swing, making proper timing much more difficult, and, if the hitter doesn't get his back elbow tucked back in on his approach, he'll cast his hands out into an unsupported position, *reducing* his power potential. (Trust me. "Been there—done that!") I know from firing-line experience at baseball's highest level, the *timing versus power* trade-off isn't worth it. *Timing* is the name of the game!

Hands to the ball? Knob to the ball? What if the pitch is outside? How does the hitter "stay inside the ball" and let his hands/knob go to the ball at the same time? It's impossible to do, but these cues are used all the time!

"Mike, How Do You Correct This Problem?"

If the rear elbow doesn't tuck in and pre-extends early in the swing, the hitter is predisposed to hit around the ball. Period. He's doomed at the outset! Tucking in the rear elbow significantly shortens the swing, allowing the player to be more compact and quicker to the ball.

During instruction, I ALWAYS have the player place the bat AGAINST his rear shoulder, with his rear elbow close to his side. When he begins his upper-body counter-rotation (pre-swing), I ask him to do so as a "unit," by *not* separating his hands from his body. This allows his hands, arms, and upper torso to retain the same relationship that he had in his stance. I then ask him to "slide" his hands through on the approach. I continue to have him repeat this until he has mastered this movement. Some become proficient more quickly than others. Once mastered, I'll ask him where HE would like to place his hands—where HE feels most comfortable and tension-free.

Again, as instructors, we should refrain from altering a player's *style*. And, in my experience, the "proper" launch position does not allow for the rear elbow to be up. But, please keep in mind, if the player IS able to keep his elbow up in the stance, and correctly tuck in his elbow by the time he gets to the launch position, let him run with it! *Every player is different.* It's just that my experience has shown it is very difficult for the younger, less mature hitter to master. When tutoring hitters, it's best to keep it as simple as possible. And, the simplest way I have found to teach this is to *totally* remove the player's "style" from the teaching equation, concentrating *solely* on the "technique."

Moreover, players who hit with their back elbow elevated also show a tendency to "wrap" their top hand. They seem to go together. By "wrapping," I mean the top hand wraps around the bat. Wrapping the top hand in this manner restricts the swing to a point where, depending on the degree of wrap, it becomes almost impossible to stay inside the ball and/or hit the inside pitch.

The correct grip involves having the top-hand "knocker-knuckles" bisecting the knuckle-set of the bottom hand. With the hands in this position, it is virtually impossible to elevate the back elbow. Correcting the position of the rear elbow often becomes one of positioning the hands properly in the player's stance.

The "Litmus" Test

As always, give yourself a "hitting litmus test." Is what I'm teaching—or being asked to do—*sound logical? Does it make sense?* If we would only take the time to do this, we could eliminate many of the incongruities, misunderstandings, and inconsistencies we encounter when teaching and learning hitting.

Our ability to articulate good information in a way hitters can internalize—and effectively use—is the most important aspect of competent coaching. Keeping it simple—and *logical*—goes a long way toward helping hitters hit their potentials.

CHAPTER 17

"The Pivotal Role of the Rear Shoulder"

I know. I know. You've "always" heard that dipping the back shoulder is a "no-no." It produces (heaven forbid!) "fly balls," a "looping swing," "chicken winging," and other mechanical unmentionables. I hear the same things you do; they've been repeated so many times we accept them as fact. I believed them, too, until I decided to ask the ultimate question: WHY? After all, this isn't what I saw all those years playing at baseball's highest level?

I can still hear Ted Williams challenging me in 1969. "Do you want to be a hitter, Mike? If you do, you've got to watch the great hitters. They'll show you all you need to know about hitting. You've got the best "seat" in the house! As a first baseman, you get to see the "open" view of every great right-handed hitter. They'll show you what you need to know; you've just got to be smart enough to see what they're showing you."

Well, I took my manager's good advice and watched intently. Hundreds of thousands of swings over a nine-year major league career. I not only saw the best American League hitters, I also got to see the best National League hitters in exhibition games during spring training—and once in the World Series.

And, even today, what I *see*—I also saw—when I played. But it seems that what we teach is a far cry from what we actually *see*. Now remember, in those days, there were no hitting coaches in the major leagues—or any "formal" instruction, for that matter. It was left to the players themselves to wade through the volumes of fact and fiction that was continually put in front of us. Possibly, one of the coaches would, from time to time, offer some advice in the form of a sagely story, perpetuating hitting's longstanding "legacy of confusion." But, the point to remember, in this instance, is that the "informational rite of passage" was principally the result of emulation, not instruction. What we did, we saw first.

The Venue Sets the Stage

It became clear that the rationale for many of the hitting cues we have used in the past have come from the changes that baseball was going through during that particular era. In the early 1970s, *Astroturf* was beginning to make its mark on major league baseball, followed by many colleges and universities. Hey, remember those days of pinball baseball in the National League? Faded fields of artificial turf with huge watermarks and stains and permanent yard markers left over from NFL games? New multi-use stadiums were being built, incorporating the new, ultra-modern "carpet." To take advantage of these "fast" playing fields, offensive baseball went through a metamorphosis. "Little ball"—"jackrabbits" running rampant on artificial turf in Cincinnati, Pittsburgh, St. Louis, Houston, Philadelphia and Montréal and keeping the ball on the ground became the rule of the day.

As usual, college and high school coaches and amateur players "copied" their professional counterparts in terms of game strategy and accompanying hitting mechanics. Scouts turned their "attention" to signing players who could "fly." Many a player was drafted with these qualifications: *"A great athlete. Can really run. Limited experience. Must teach him to hit."* Teaching him to hit was to teach him to put the ball in play—on the ground— and run like hell.

Astroturf infields were so fast, infielders couldn't catch up to ground balls. "Beat an infielder" was the daily advice. We were taught to swing down, which *automatically* predisposed our weight to come on to the front side. This went on for about twenty years. Accordingly, we entered baseball's "Jack Rabbit Era." *Hands and arms hitters, speed, contact, ground balls*, and *"little ball"* became instant buzzwords. *Staying back, power, working the count,* and *high slugging percentages* were out. A terrific club, managed by a wonderful manager, Whitey Herzog (a former manager of mine), the world champion St. Louis Cardinals of the mid '80s, epitomized this trend.

The Dawn of a New Era

Today, it's a new era. Only a few major league teams still have plastic playing surfaces, and nearly all colleges and universities have reverted back to natural grass. (After this year, only Tampa Bay in the AL may still have artificial turf.)

Astroturf, diving, getting the weight to the front side, and *swinging down* are now dinosaurs of the past. We're in a "new-old" age of hitting. We've gone back to pre-aluminum bat mechanics, back to the days of baseball's "Golden Offensive Era" (1920-1970), and the upsurge in hitting at the major league level has been breathtaking.

As coaches, we must be able to see and understand these changes taking place today. Because the players *already* see them and are copying them. Even if you aren't *teaching* them, your productive hitters are already *doing* them.

Has YOUR Teaching Philosophy Changed?

To start, please ask yourself this question: "Do I currently teach the cues 'stay back' or 'keep your weight back?'" *If you do*, like it or not, you are a part of the current hitting metamorphosis. Whether or not you are willing to recognize and acknowledge this is immaterial. The fact remains that up until a few years ago, you were probably teaching linear mechanics. "Hit off your front foot" and "let your weight come forward" were likely your teaching mantras. And, why not? After all, you were simply teaching players to take advantage of the new venue: ultra-light aluminum bats and the rock-hard *Astroturf* playing surfaces.

But, I think it is important that we don't lose our sense of history here. It is noteworthy that *95% of baseball's Hall of Fame hitters kept their weight back*. "Lunging" has always been something to avoid at all costs.

For over one hundred years, players and coaches have understood that lunging drastically dissipates bat speed and power in the swing. And yet, the aluminum bats made it possible to overcome this physical and biomechanical curse. Not any more; the minus 3s and natural grass have seen to that. Today's hitter cannot not let his weight come forward, if he is to be productive and hit his potential.

Those of you who continue to teach linear mechanics and the concept of "front-foot hitting" may have no use for this article. For most others, it will be a blessing, because it will show you how to restrain your hitters from lunging, the curse of every *productive* hitter that ever played the game of baseball.

Why Players Lunge

Hitters lunge because they are the sum total of what they have been taught. As a hitting instructor, I have always considered myself the "caretaker" of my students' hitting mechanics. When I look at a player, I see a "computer," something that has the ability and resources to do wonderful things. To fully realize their inherent potential, computers must be *programmed* with software that provides a solid blueprint for its many tasks.

The *quality* of the software we use to program a computer is commensurate with that of the player and his own personal software, which ultimately becomes integral to his success or failure. This software becomes his *blueprint* from which all his mechanical movements originate and take place. I call this software his *technique*.

Hitters are born with "natural" swings. The ideal—and most efficient—software is inherently built-in. Then, when youngsters become old enough to begin tee ball, coaches "re-program" them to *swing down, squish the bug, watch the ball hit the bat, and not to dip the back shoulder.*

Improper programming (coaching) and second-rate software (technique) predispose many youngsters to failure from the get-go, and is one of the primary reasons why baseball loses so many good athletes to other sports. Few tasks are as athletically demanding as hitting a baseball.

"Don't dip the back shoulder" has been a major contributor to the lunging epidemic that runs rampant with linear mechanics. Accordingly, this cue becomes the linchpin for any discussion concerning lunging, because lunging CANNOT be corrected *without* the dipping of the back shoulder!

Okay, Mike, How Do We Correct This Problem?

If a player lunges, it's generally because he can. He has been *programmed* to swing down (and thus geared for coming on to the front side). When a player's front heel drops to initiate his swing, the rear shoulder must dip (assuming, of course, the pitch isn't letters-high or above). I tell students it's like having "a taut rope tied from your front heel to your back shoulder." When the front heel drops, the "rope" simultaneously "pulls" the back shoulder down where it should be. As this is occurring, the lead elbow begins to work *up*. When this happens, the player's weight stabilizes on the inside of his REAR thigh. *A hitter must be programmed to effectuate this critical move* (either through emulation or formal instruction). If not, he will be predisposed to coming forward and lunging. It's that simple.

Photo credit: Rick Stewart/Allsport

Barry Bonds' swing approach. Notice how his "shoulder dip" stabilizes his weight on the inside of his rear thigh.

Bernie Williams is a line-drive gap hitter, so he is more upright on his axis than the "pure-power" hitter.

The degree to which the player "tilts" back on the axis determines the gradient of the swing. For the pure power hitter, such as Barry Bonds, he will sit back further off the axis than perhaps, a line-drive gap hitter, such as Bernie Williams. Players with less power will/should be more upright on their axis; they will utilize a "flatter" swing gradient. *The more upright a player is on his axis, the greater will be his predisposition to come forward during his swing.* The goal for the majority of hitters should be line drives. This objective normally dictates staying slightly *behind* the axis and dipping the rear shoulder. If the player has some power, he'll get his share of round trippers and extra-base hits.

However, pitches that are "up" in the strike zone (e.g., at the letters), the degree of "tilt" (and shoulder dip) lessens as the player raises his hands to get on top of the pitch and "level off" the swing. As a result, his weight can/will come forward in the absence of a distinct rearward body tilt.

Ted Williams used to caution me and my Washington Senators teammates to "set our sights higher" if the high pitch was giving one of us trouble. He'd say, "think about getting your hands on top of the ball more." This advice implies "anticipation" in its most exacting definition. Even if you "look" (anticipate) for the high pitch, your mechanics shouldn't change. Your hips should still lead the hands, and you must stay inside the ball. The only difference would be the positioning of your swing plane relative to the plane of the incoming pitch.

On the other hand, pitches that are "down" at the knees will necessitate a more pronounced shoulder dip to enable the hitter to "match the plane of the swing to the plane of the pitch." In other words, *the extent to which the rear shoulder dips ultimately depends on the pitch's horizontal location in the contact zone.*

The hitter's initial swing plane is "roughed out" when his rear shoulder dips. This "tilting" movement insures a swing gradient "close" to what the hitter perceives the pitch plane to be coming out of the pitcher's hand. Once he determines this, which is based on the reference he has picked up from previous like-pitches to the same area, he then predicts where his bat will make contact in his hitting zone, relative to the prediction he has made on where the incoming pitch will be. Above all else, HITTING IS PREDICTION. And, this prediction is based on information the hitter has collected in previous at-bats against this particular pitcher.

This hitter "analysis" is performed in lightning-quick fashion, unbeknownst to the hitter actually performing the task. It's like "ram memory" in a computer. It takes place in nanoseconds and stays there until its capacity is reached and newer information dislodges it. The larger the ram memory, the longer the information stays there. That's why I say "a hitter has to be strong to compete—but smart to win." Only HE can determine the size and effective use of his ram memory!

Two Questions That Can Help!

The following two questions can immeasurably help a coach's analysis:

❏ *Is the player dipping his rear shoulder immediately after his front heel drops?* Again, the cue I use is to tell the player that he should "feel" a rope—stretched tight—running from his front heel to his rear shoulder. When the player drops his front heel, the imaginary "rope" should "pull down" his rear shoulder, as his front heel drops.

❏ *Is the player "tilting" correctly and getting his lead elbow up in time?* This is one of the key points to look for! This singular movement can stop linear movement dead in its tracks! When the player's front heel drops, his rear shoulder must begin to dip at nearly the same instant. As this is happening, the player's rear elbow must begin to tuck in close to his body, allowing his lead elbow to begin working up. This "tilting" movement will automatically place the player's weight to the INSIDE of his rear thigh, precluding any forward movement.

"I Never See a Hitter Drop His Back Shoulder!"

To that I always say, "only to those who harbor preconceived biases and what I call *selective vision*" can such a statement be true. However, in the real world of hitting, the fact is every productive hitter that's ever played the game of baseball drops his back shoulder. *He has to!* If he doesn't, he will lunge, thereby mitigating any proper physical moves he has made up to that point.

The following photos illustrate a few examples of this factor. While we may still be teaching "level shoulders," the fact is that our productive hitters are already copying their major league brethren. It's there for anyone to see. Emulation is a very powerful teaching tool.

Larry Walker.

Note back shoulder and its favorable impact on keeping the hitter from coming forward.

Ken Griffey, Jr.

Note back shoulder and its favorable impact on keeping the hitter from coming forward.

Matt Williams.

Note back shoulder and its favorable impact on keeping the hitter from coming forward.

Mike's Coaching Tip: Balance. Balance. Balance.

It is important that the coach remember that to teach proper mechanics effectively, the player must re-gain the balance point in his stride, because without proper preparation (balance), the dynamic sequencing of the upper and lower torsos (torque) goes for naught; it is virtually impossible to rotate the hips optimally using only "one" leg. *Proper rotation requires both legs balanced to ensure maximum rotational velocity.*

In addition, if the player holds too much weight on his back leg when he strides, and it "collapses" as he launches his swing, his swing gradient can become TOO steep, creating the "looping swing" alluded to at the beginning of this article. Make no mistake here: swinging "up" too much is just as bad as swinging "down" too much.

The "Window of Opportunity"

During the off-season, I'll assist professional players who must correct their drifting problem. My reputation is that I can get this "done" in a matter of days. It sure beats the emulation process, which could take years—provided the player even has the ability to internalize what he sees. Neither the player's agent nor the player can wait that long. By that time, their window of opportunity could very well have passed them by. This should hold true for hitters at any age and level.

Being able to understand the "whys" of lunging—and having the knowledge to correct it—will enable the coach to easily eliminate this mechanical defect. Not only will it improve your overall team offense, but you will also be helping your individual players hit their potentials. Either way, *everyone* comes out a winner!

CHAPTER 18

"The 'No-Stride' Approach"

The no-stride approach is gaining widespread popularity with players desiring to become more "compact" and "quicker" to the ball. One area of concern with coaches, however, is the potential loss of both power and bat speed as a direct result of not striding.

Actually, as you will see, the *length* of a player's stride—or even the very *absence* of a stride—has absolutely *nothing* to do with the amount of power or bat speed that a hitter generates!

As an instructor, it makes no difference to me *how* a hitter strides. While I prefer the no-stride approach, or at least, a very short stride, the decision is ultimately dependent on the hitter himself. In other words, it has to *be* right—and *feel* right—for the hitter if he is to hit his potential.

Why Hitters Stride

Hitters stride for a variety of reasons, most notably to *break inertia, to set up an axis of rotation (AOR), and to re-establish the balance point in their swing. Breaking inertia* is the hitter's way of "getting started." It is very difficult for a hitter to hit from a stand-still position. (For the same reason, pitchers use a windup.) Preliminary movement gives the hitter a "head start" for the task-at-hand. I don't remember seeing many successful hitters in the major leagues that didn't move rhythmically before pitch release. Other ways exist to describe breaking inertia, including "rhythm," dancing with the pitcher, and turn your back to the pitcher when he turns his back to you. No matter how it is conveyed to the hitter, he must understand the cornerstone role that "getting started" plays in the good swing.

The hitter must also set up an *axis of rotation* (AOR) in his stride. The AOR provides an imaginary "pole" around which his body will rotate. Once the hitter strides and sets up his AOR, when his front heel drops, *his head does not move forward* as he rotates around his axis. If it does, he is drifting.

Re-establishing the balance point is also an integral component of the correct swing. A common coaching cue used today is "load up." This is *in vogue*, because we are trying to get our players to "stay back"—not "come forward," which was yesterday's buzzword. I find that if the player is taught to load up in his stance—and doesn't *regain* the balance point in his stride, the amount of weight he holds on his back side will flow in an equal amount to his front side as he swings, *sustaining* the lunging condition. Or, equally as bad, he will collapse his back side, yielding a too-steep gradient to his swing. Balance means 50-50. For the player not to lunge, he MUST regain the balance point in his stride, and maintain it when he launches his swing. However, *"loading up" is acceptable, as long as the hitter regains the balance point when he strides.*

Balance is the Key

The goal of every instructor/player should be a "repeatable" swing, and balance is a prerequisite for this condition. Rotational hitting mechanics beg for balance; one cannot rotate correctly—or effectively—on one leg! Balance maximizes a hitter's rotational velocity and is linked directly to bat quickness (launch-to-contact) and bat speed. There should be no question as to its importance to successful hitting.

The human body persistently searches for its own personal "balance point." When we are "balanced," we feel "comfortable" and "in control." In the same way, balance is also integral to good hitting, and many coaches use the "balance" cue when tutoring hitters. When we walk, our body "finds" its balance point, although we are not consciously aware of it; it has become natural and "second nature" to us. In effect, walking is *dynamic balance* in action. It is why, when we see babies learning to walk, it is a constant battle with balance, until their bodies—through trial and error—figure it out. When we see people walking, we see many different styles. Yet, while they may *appear* different to us, they're all utilizing the same *walking technique* (one foot before the other).

In addition, the *length* of everyone's *walking stride* is different and personal to that individual. Since hitters *should* be dynamically balanced in their swings, their bodies will naturally attempt to find their proper balance points, unless someone (their coach?) physically teaches something different. Personally, I can't remember seeing a hitter lose his balance during his swing and saying to myself, "Wow! What a *beautiful* swing!" If it isn't *cosmetically* beautiful, it probably isn't *functionally* beautiful either, and a far cry from where it should be.

If a hitter always seeks his balance point, and his walking stride IS his own personal balance point, I have found that he will attempt to get there on every swing. Even if the hitter has a very "narrow" stance, say, his feet are 12-inches apart, and his *walking stride* is 34 inches, his *batting stride* will make up this difference. Why? Because *his balance point is his comfort zone.* I have also found that the length of a player's bat is very close to the length of his actual walking stride. (I'm talking high school players on up in this instance.)

A mature player's optimum stride is normally the length of his bat.

If this is the case, shouldn't it follow that a hitter should spread his feet to this balance-point length in his stance? (See photo.) If he does, then, theoretically, he would have no "reason" to stride. He's already at his optimum pre-swing base-position—and is balanced as well!

Lining Up the Feet

When instructing hitters, I teach the "feet-square" approach, meaning both feet are in line with the plate—neither open, nor closed. It is more difficult for a pitcher to get a "read" on the hitter than if he is open or closed. Emulation dictates that most players copy the big leaguers, and today, they are seeing many of them with open stances.

I've always been intrigued by hitters who say they have open stances to get a "better look" at the pitcher. But, curiously, as they *close down* to *square up* in the pre-swing, they position their head to where it *would* have been had they had a square stance to begin with! This is a product of their style, not their technique, and a way for them "to get started." If a hitter is comfortable with an open stance, is getting to the proper launch position on time, and is getting results, then let him run with it. Players should just make sure they understand *why* they are doing this: it is for breaking inertia and creating some rhythm in their swing.

However, my experience dictates that if a hitter is going to have an open stance, he would be wise to stay open. If he starts closed, stay closed. Starts square, stay square. Players that start open, and then close down in the stride (leave the original heel line) have a more difficult time getting their hips through. When pitchers see this type hitter, they try to pitch them inside and jam them, because of the difficulty many hitters have when closing down their hips in the stride. Conversely, if the hitter starts closed or square, but strides open, pitchers will pitch him away. Hitters, especially younger hitters, should stay on their original heel line for good plate coverage and optimum hip rotation. Hitters need to find their own comfort level, and this is done by developing their own personal style through *trial and error.*

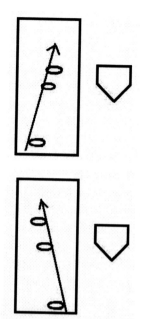

Stay on the "heel line."

Why a No-Stride Approach?

The same criteria used for the normal-stride approach (*breaking inertia, setting up an axis of rotation, and re-establishing the balance point*) also apply to the no-stride approach. In addition, *compactness, staying on the heel line, optimum stride length,* and *very little head movement* are added benefits of the no-stride approach. But remember, it is *not* for everyone, because we are talking about the potential variances in style (comfort) here.

Coaches talk glowingly about good hitters being "compact." (Barry Bonds is a good example.) Eliminating the stride takes the term "compactness" to a higher level. Remember my cue? *Less is more.*

The no-stride approach eliminates the potential for the hitter to come off the heel line, which means less head movement. And, by widening his base to get into his optimum balanced position, the hitter is also lowering his *center of gravity.* This is very important, because it also positions the hitter's head closer to the point of impact. These benefits makes it easier to focus on the pitch.

Another advantage to the hitter lowering his center of gravity is that it positions his body in an impossible-to-move position. The player's base is too wide, and his center of gravity is too low to permit his body to "give" at contact. If a player's base is too narrow, the same does not hold true. At contact, ANY "give" at all in a hitter's hands and/or body will dissipate power in the swing.

The shorter the stride, the less head movement there is in the swing. One of the distinguishing characteristics of the poorly designed swing is having *multiple* objects moving simultaneously: the head and the ball. It is impossible for the hitter to control the movement of the pitch, but he CAN control the movement of his head. Being able to absolutely concentrate/focus on the pitch is crucial to successful hitting.

Teaching the No-Stride Approach

With the normal-stride approach, as the hitter strides, he counter-rotates his upper torso rearward (*winds the rubber band*), followed *immediately* by striding and opening his front foot. His front foot should open up to at least 45 degrees, and he *must land with his heel off the ground*. Dropping the front heel triggers the swing. In the correct rotational swing, there is no swing until the front heel drops.

Now, in the no-stride approach, the hitter must also have his front foot open to at least 45 degrees. However, instead of striding, his feet are initially placed in the desired "balance-point" position (approximately equal to the length of his bat). This will preclude any tendency for him to want to stride any more; he's already at his body's ideal balance point. As the pitch comes in, he counter-rotates his upper torso (*winds the rubber band*), SIMULTANEOUSLY as he takes his front knee *inward*. The hitter must NOT change the position of his front foot. In other words, he must keep it at the same angle he had previously set up in his stance.

This counter-rotational movement will cause the front heel to rise up, placing the hitter in the *identical* position as the hitter who took the normal-stride approach. (*He should not just lift the foot up and set it down in one motion.*) He then drops his heel to trigger his swing. Additionally, opening his front foot in the stance will allow his hips to open and come through naturally.

The dropping of the heel, coupled with the counter-rotating upper torso, creates "torque," which is the foundation for bat speed and power in the baseball swing. As the "linkage" between the upper and lower torsos "tighten," the forward momentum of the largest muscle mass in the hitter's body (his legs) "yank" the smaller muscles (his hands and arms) through the strike zone. When we use the cue, *pop the hips*, this is what we are really saying; these are the correct biomechanical movements needed to effectuate it.

The key is getting the front heel off the ground. When it drops, it triggers the swing. Joe DiMaggio, Paul Molitor, Nomar Garciaparra, and Jim Edmonds are but a few of the many players who have had wonderful success without striding. Although they look different, you clearly see them raising the heel of their stride foot off the ground and displaying identical techniques.

At the launch position, both the normal-stride and no-stride approaches mirror one another. They are *identical*, except the no-stride hitter did very little to get there!

Mike's Coaching Tip: Counter-Rotate as a "Unit."

Coaches should make sure the player's upper-half (torso, hands, and arms) counter-rotate as a "unit." The elbows should be "soft" (i.e., "bent"), until full extension occurs slightly before contact.

Got It, Mike, But WHEN Does the Heel Drop?

We should now know, that in rotational hitting, the hitter's front heel "triggers" his swing. And, if he doesn't get his front heel down *on time*, he will have no "choice" but to be late. This is a *personal choice* made by the hitter, and is dependent on many factors, notwithstanding a hitter's personal resources, correctly anticipating the pitch, the quality of his mechanics, and the velocity of the pitch.

Hitters with "poor" mechanics must start their swing earlier than those whose mechanics are short to the ball and compact. The front heel normally drops when the pitch is *approximately* 15' in front of the plate. I have an old clip of Babe Ruth taken from the top of an old rickety grandstand in St. Louis in the 1920s, showing a situation where he dropped his front heel when the oncoming pitch was about 10' in front of the plate and STILL pulled a line drive base hit between first and second! It's different for *everyone*—but the hitter must make sure he gets his heel down on *time!*

I tell players daily that "less is more" in baseball. We get into trouble when we try to do too much; too many things can go wrong! This also applies to the striding sequence. Personally, I would rather my hitters be as short and compact to the ball as possible, with minimum head movement. When a player strides, his head must also move forward. Having two variables (the head and the ball) moving at the same time is much more difficult to overcome than simply focusing solely on the pitch. I have had far greater results incorporating this into my instruction. That's just my experience and preference; other individuals have their own opinions.

As for a loss of power, I hope you are able to see that this factor should not be an issue. In the no-stride approach, the hitter gets to the *identical* launch position as the player who takes a stride. Dropping the front heel initiates the separation of the upper and lower torsos and applies torque to the swing. Regardless of the stride approach a hitter uses, without torque, bat quickness and power quickly dissipate.

The type of stride a hitter uses should be based on his style and comfort level. Imposing the coach's own personal comfort values on a hitter can be the first step in a continuing progression of failures. Whether the hitter strides—or doesn't stride—should be his decision—and his alone.

CHAPTER 19

"Flat-Palm Hitting"

Flat-palm hitting is an often-used term that relates to the hitter's hands when the swing goes ballistic. The hands are then put into this advantageous position through a simple *torquing process*. Correctly using "flat-palm hitting" is fundamental to productive hitting and certain hitting *types*. However, over the past twenty five years, its correct definition has become badly distorted. In this article you will find that the problem most hitters incur is *not* the results of swinging down, but rather, taking the downward plane of the swing *too far*.

What is "Flat-Palm Hitting?"

"Flat-palm hitting" is the ability of the hitter, when launching his swing, to get his hands quickly into a position parallel to the ground. Most struggling players who come for instruction do not do this. When launching their swing, they show me a position where their hands are nearly perpendicular to the ground. This is the reality of linear mechanics which aluminum bats have fostered and nurtured since the early 1970s.

A by-product of the linear technique has been a "swing-down-through-the-ball" approach. When players are instructed to swing down, their hands never get to the desired flat-palm position until well past their front knee, if at all.

History is Made on the Inside-Half of the Plate!

Previously, I talked about Ted Williams' classic statement that "history is made on the inside-half of the plate." A *flat-palm* hitting approach is essential if the hitter is to take advantage of this Williams *gem*.

The anatomy of the *natural* baseball swing is such, that when a swing is launched, its initial plane is somewhat down. This *slight* downward plane continues until it is within 3"-5" *of the lead knee*, where it begins to level off and *begins its slight upslope as it passes the lead knee.* The slight upslope then continues until the player has finished his follow-through. From the side—or "open" view of the hitter, we see the classic *shallow* "U," as the hands go down slightly out of the launch position, level off for a short period, and then rise as the swing progresses toward follow-through.

Where pitches are contacted can make a difference in the ball's off-the-bat exit trajectories. To hit pitches on the outer-half of the plate, the player *must* wait for the ball to get "deep." When he does this correctly, he contacts the pitch in the slightly downward plane of his swing. This imparts a lower trajectory to the pitches he hits. Conversely, to hit the pitch middle-half in, the player *must* hit the pitch out in front of his lead knee—or else he won't get his arms extended, and he'll get jammed. The path of his swing in this desirable hitting area is slightly up.

The hitter's body always delivers *maximum* momentum and energy in the area out in *front* of his lead knee. Williams' logical conclusion was "why do I want to waste a swing at a pitch in this explosive area by hitting a ground ball?" He reasoned this is the area to "wreak havoc." He was right; so were 95% of baseball's Hall of Fame hitters, who have been creating mayhem in the same area for over one hundred years.

Today's *dominant* hitters perpetuate Williams' keen insight into this hands/contact phenomenon. While it is true not every hitter can dominate, my belief is that few hit their potentials. Many singles/contact types *could* become more productive by incorporating better technique into swings. This is one of them. Hopefully, you now understand that *how far the hitter takes the initial downward plane of his swing often makes the difference between "power and production" or "singles and contact."*

If *flat-palm hitting* has benefited so many outstanding hitters down through the years, why do we teach something altogether different? Do we teach what we really see?

Mike's Coaching Sidebar

Many hitting coaches teach hitters that they must go down and get the low pitch or else they won't hit it. Actually, nothing could be further from reality. Restricting an extended downward plane should be the goal for most hitting types. Coaches should know that the barrel of the bat is ALWAYS below the hands at contact, unless the player swings at a pitch at his armpits (or above). For this reason, the hands do not have to drop way down to hit the low strike. The barrel of the bat will find the ball; the hands should return to approximately the same spot each time. The hitter's eye-hand coordination then takes over!

The "Torques"

Initially, flat-palm hitting is a torquing process, so let's define torque once again for those individuals who may not fully understand the term. Put simply and understandably, *torque is two forces working simultaneously—in opposite directions—on an object.* Anytime this relationship is set up in physical movement, torque is the result.

The good rotational swing goes through a number of "torques" as it becomes ballistic. One distinct, undeniable torque in the rotational swing is the separation of the upper and lower torsos (*"hips lead hands"*), that occurs when the stride heel plants. This singular movement is the foundation for all bat speed, bat quickness, and power in the swing. Another torque is the result of the hitter quickly *flattening out* his hands as he launches his swing. The hands flatten out, as the top hand pulls down, and the bottom hand pulls up. These two diametrically opposed forces work on the bat, producing *torque*. This also has an enhancing effect on bat speed and potential power, and is the result of the hands flattening out as the swing launches.

Ted Williams used to tell hitters that if they wanted to be good, they better "watch the good ones." In his own inimitable way, he got his point across. As a big league first baseman, I had the best seat in the house, watching the "open view" of every great right-handed hitter who played in the American League from 1966-74, including some in the National League during spring training. Watching these great hitters all those years left an indelible impression on my mind, not only with their intelligent mindsets in specific hitting counts and game situations, but also with their hitting movements. Unlike the blurred, hardly noticeable torquing of the upper and lower torsos, the flattening of the hands out of the launch position was clearly visible and easy to see.

Why is "Flat-Palm Hitting" Important?

Flat-palm hitting is important for shaping the plane of the hitter's swing. As many of you will recall, my definition of the "perfect swing" is *the adjustment the hitter makes to the pitch he gets.*

All pitches are thrown in a downward plane, and the vast majority of these pitches are at the knees. For this reason, the hitter *must* learn how to make the proper adjustment to the oncoming pitch. This is accomplished by "tilting" his body to accommodate the plane of the oncoming pitch. Tilting the body, coupled with flattening the hands, allows the hitter to do this.

Learning this may require physically placing the player in the correct positions, or through emulation. For many, it is 180° from what has been taught since they started playing "organized" baseball. A list of the misguided cues includes *swing down, ground balls are good, beat an infielder, there's no errors on fly balls, et al.* Swinging down *was* the name of the game. Following these cues have resulted in hitters taking the downward-plane phase of the swing "too far."

The productive hitter is once again learning to *flatten out* his hands as quickly as possible. Executing the *flat-palms* approach correctly will facilitate the more desirable goal of "matching the plane of his swing to the plane of the oncoming pitch." Unfortunately, hitters are learning it through emulation, rather than coaching. Good coaching always gets quicker results.

Photo credit: Jeff Gross/AllspOrt

Notice Barry Bonds' flat-to-slightly-up hand position at contact.

Today, as hitting mechanics change from *linear* to *rotational*, a better understanding on the part of coaches is necessary to extract the hitter's potential. If we teach a *pre-determined* swing plane to our players, we restrict the *natural* tendency of the player to make the on-the-fly adjustment needed to increase contact. And, sadly, many of us inadvertently do just that!

Quickly getting the top-hand underneath facilitates this on-the-fly transitioning. But, if the player is taught to swing down *only*, he loses this essential flexibility. He's programmed to do one thing only, thus restricting his ability to naturally adjust to the oncoming pitch.

What Hitting Types Use "Flat-Palm Hitting?"

The degree to which different *hitting types* use "flat palms" can vary. If you recall, I classify hitters according to types: *singles/contact, line-drive/gap, and pure power.* As might be expected, the pure power hitter (for example, Barry Bonds) would need to get his top-hand underneath more quickly and tilt back more than the singles/contact hitter (e.g., Ichiro Suzuki and Tony Gwynn). *Getting the top hand underneath works hand-in-hand with the amount of body tilt generated in the approach phase.*

Ichiro Suzuki

Photo credit: Otto Greule, Jr./Allsport

Photo credit: Gary Newkirk/AllspOrt

Tony Gwynn

With no (or negative) body tilt, the singles/contact type of hitter, like Ichiro, would have a more difficult time working the top hand underneath, and would take the downward plane of his swing further than the line-drive/gap (e.g., Derek Jeter) or pure power types. Singles/contact hitters want a flatter or more downward swing gradient.

I hope you can also see, at this point, that a hitter gets very little *hand-torque* by swinging down, or chopping down at the ball. On the other hand, one should also be able to see that by flattening the hands immediately at swing launch, this condition is greatly enhanced. It is another reason why linear hitters have not hit for power and production over the years.

Beware of "Barring!"

Perhaps it's a part of *Americana*, meaning that "if a little is good, more must be better!" It certainly seems to be the case with *hand torque*. Make sure your hitters do not preliminarily "cock" their bottom wrist so much that it sends the bat head pointing back toward the pitcher. This produces a *long swing* and can significantly hamper good *timing* and *staying inside the ball*.

Cocking the bottom wrist, in an attempt to produce *more* hand torque at the launch position, can have very detrimental effects if not performed correctly. A hitter's main objective is to be short and compact! Cocking the bottom wrist can pre-dispose the hitter's lead arm to straighten out, yielding a barred-out condition. This will lead to hitting around the ball.

Now, granted, there have been a number of terrific hitters down through the years who have barred their lead arm out of the launch position. However, they also have been athletically gifted enough to stay inside the ball in the approach phase of the swing *and arrive on time*. For those few that can do it, there are probably a jillion hitters we never heard of because they DID this very same thing—and got nowhere.

I'm not saying that an individual can't hit this way. I work with big leaguers down through younger players. And, while the pros invariably are more mature physically, more experienced, and have more advanced motor coordination (i.e., more resources), it puts many younger players at a real disadvantage. A hitter will have AMPLE *hand torque* without cocking his bottom wrist.

Okay, Mike, How Do You Teach It?

Does a hitter have to know the role that *flat-palm hitting* plays in the swing? I don't believe he does. In the good rotational swing, it happens *automatically*. When the front heel plants to initiate hip rotation, there is the simultaneous movement of the upper-body "tilt." This tilting movement lowers the rear shoulder somewhat. The rear elbow tucks in "hard" against the body, and the lead elbow works up. The hard elbow "tuck," out of the launch position, is the key! This tilting movement "automatically" begins flattening the bat and torquing the hands.

Attempting to specifically teach this goes beyond my definition of tutoring hitting mechanics as simply and understandably as possible. However, if a player is having a problem, there are some cues that I have used successfully. My subjective cue for teaching this is *drop (the heel) and tilt*. My more specific, objective cues in this instance are *scoop sand with the top hand, tuck the back elbow, and get your hands as flat as you can—as quick as you can*. By so doing, the player should automatically flatten his hands and initiate his hand torque. Does the player have to know why? No. He just needs to be able to do it – correctly. (My videotape set, "Do We Teach What

We Really See?" contains the proprietary drills necessary for the player to assume all of the proper positions he needs.)

Benefits of *"Flat-Palm Hitting"*

There are many benefits that accrue from this swing event, including: an increase in bat speed, aiding the rear elbow to *slot* correctly, allowing the lead elbow to seamlessly work *up*, provides for the vital body *tilt*, naturally places the hitter's weight on the inside of his *rear thigh*, and helps promote "matching the plane of the swing to the plane of the pitch." These valuable benefits fully warrant the coach/hitter to understand, learn, and implement *flat-palm hitting* into their coaching philosophy, so it will become a normal, reactive part of the swing.

Some individuals believe that flattening the hands at the launch position leads to increased bat speed, and perhaps more power. I would not dispute this. I know I used hand torque when I played. But, if a hitter is going to use it, he better be able to control it! And many young players can't. And not being able to control it can easily lead to a pre-extended condition of the lead elbow (casting), excessive bottom hand "cocking," and a "long" swing. We see a few big leaguers do it every day on the TV screen, so we're tempted to copy them. But, these are "world-class" athletes. My personal opinion is *I would not trade "staying inside the ball" for a few extra mph on my swing—or a few extra feet on a fly ball*. Having a long swing and trying to stay inside the ball with a barred-out lead arm are inconceivable for the average player and are highly restraining for the elite player.

Getting the hitter to effectuate this torquing movement, and the ensuing flattening of the hands, can have a very positive impact on the baseball swing's quickness, power, and production. It's certainly worth the effort.

CHAPTER 20

"The Important Role of Leverage: The Body" (Part #1)

After Ted Williams' passing, we all read testimonials from baseball's elite hitters and other players who said, "We all tried to copy him; he had flawless mechanics." Hall of Famer Eddie Collins once watched Williams' form in batting practice and immediately declared it the most perfect he had ever seen, better even than that of the great "Shoeless" Joe Jackson. Collins made this observation in 1936. At the time, Williams was 17 years old.

I have often wondered why so many great hitters have embraced these very same mechanics for their singular success, yet so few coaches show any regard for the remarkable results they have produced over the past 100 years. Many coaches have little or no inclination to teach them. People say it's too difficult to teach, *but it really isn't*. They say Williams was the *only* player who could hit that way, *but he really wasn't*. In fact, 95% of baseball's Hall of Fame hitters used *the very same technique*, including today's best hitters! In a recent newspaper article, for-sure Hall of Famer Tony Gwynn made some interesting comments about a conversation he had with Williams in 1992. The following are some excerpts from the article:

GWYNN: "Ted [Williams] changed my game. Ted really ragged on me. He looked at my 31-ounce bat and called it a toothpick. He thought a guy my size should be driving the ball more and using a bigger bat. It was the first time somebody like that had really gotten on me. And, I found I really liked it. Because, it wasn't like you were just hearing another tip from another player. It's like you were getting preached to by the bishop of a church. At first, it was more a matter of me being in awe of Ted Williams. But then I started to absorb the things he was saying. For years I'd hit the ball to left [opposite field] and be satisfied. He showed me different."

WILLIAMS: "Son, major league history's made on the ball inside. You show them you can handle that ball, then they'll throw it out where you want it. They won't pitch you inside."

GWYNN: "*Handle* is hitting it out of the ball park. *Handle* is taking a guy's best heater on the inside and pulling it down the (right-field) line, *hard.* I always had the kind of stroke where it was hard getting the barrel head out in front, I had the kind of swing that was good *to* the ball, but not *through* the ball."

NEWS WRITER: "How very ironic…that when Gwynn finally began driving the ball the way Williams had suggested, he suddenly was the greatest threat to Williams' exalted status as the last .400 hitter. Not since then, has Gwynn finished any season lower than .321."

When so many players with big league "firing-line" experience say Williams had hitting's best mechanics, wouldn't it make sense to teach them? I have come to the conclusion that many coaches don't want to take the time to learn to teach them. Sadly, the players become the real losers for their coaches lackadaisical indifference. Too many of us have a tendency to adopt the "if I'm not teaching it, it's wrong" mentality. They then turn their back on the problem, hoping it will just go "away."

NOW I See It!

Many of you have thanked me for exposing physical movements in the baseball swing that have long been unrecognized because they happen so quickly, sometimes in micro-instants. Wade Boggs, in a *Sports Illustrated* article years ago, said, "It was unbelievable, just talking hitting (with Ted Williams) the whole night. When he asked me about smelling the bat burning, I told him I never had. Well, the very next day I fouled off a pitch, and I smelled the burning wood. I just never noticed before Ted brought it up. I must have smelled it 300 times over the rest of my career. But, up until that night, I never had paid attention to it."

Since pointing out a number of these swing nuances in my videos and articles, many people have said they *now* see them every night on ESPN. They were there before, guys—we just didn't know what we were looking for! I *know* your players see them; most are already doing them.

In order to teach hitting effectively, we must teach what we *really* see; not what we *want* to see. But, first, we must know *what* to look for.

Logic is the Key

Logic should always rule our tutoring, but many times, we simply parrot information we hear, because we do not know *what* to look for.

I'm sure you've noticed that I make it a point to tell you how grateful I am to the many unselfish players, coaches, and colleagues, past and present, who have contributed to my hitting education. In essence, I am communicating their wisdom to you "standing on their broad shoulders." My enduring task in this regard has been to crystallize this mountain of already-known fact and fiction in a way that makes sense—and can be readily taught. From your overwhelming acceptance, I trust this has met with your approval.

In addition, I tell you that my only goal is to make you THINK. Does the information I am presenting sound LOGICAL? Does it make SENSE? If I can somehow persuade you to simply ASK these simple questions, then I feel like I have succeeded. Because, ultimately, it will make us all collectively smarter—and "better" at what we do, which is winning games and helping our players hit their potentials.

Lou Pavlovich, *Collegiate Baseball News'* esteemed editor and publisher, and I chatted after the N.C.A.A. World Series in Omaha. He said that he was "amazed" at how many players and coaches read my hitting articles and had embraced the hitting mechanics that I advocate. "I only saw maybe 4-5 players in the WHOLE tournament who didn't do what you say happens in the swing," he said.

I told him I thought his observations might have been somewhat misleading, that it was more that the teams that *didn't* use these mechanics ever got that far! In other words, only teams with quality hitting programs get to the CWS. If you go out and watch the quality baseball programs at both high schools and colleges, you'll see the greatest percentage of hitters staying back, rotating, and "matching the plane of their swings to the plane of the pitch."

We're Getting Smarter!

Despite some random blips on the screen, we're finally starting to question things. Do we really *want* hitters to be swinging "down" at pitches going "down?" When we "match the plane of the swing to the plane of the pitch," we're able to counteract and thwart the goal of the pitchers. Whatever pitchers do, hitters have to adjust and do the opposite. I explain it by simply saying, "hitters must 'tilt' to avoid the 'tilt.'"

Photo credit: Doug Pensinger/Getty Images

Chipper Jones is playing perfect form, matching swing plane with pitch plane.

Derek Jeter, a line drive/gap-type hitter will not tilt back as far as a pure-power type, but more than a singles/contact-type hitter.

Put another way, the hitter must counteract the downward "tilt" of the pitch by "tilting" his body rearward on his swing approach, so he can initially get on the plane of the pitch. The lower the pitch, the greater the hitter's body tilt. And vice versa. This is what productive hitting is all about, and is a principal reason why baseball's elite hitters manage to hit their POTENTIAL—and also why so many other players leave the game prematurely and never realize their lifelong dream. The "tilt" is accomplished by exerting leverage in the swing.

I can assure you that your players see pictures of good hitters and are emulating their movements, *despite what you may be teaching them*. As coaches, we must get on the "band wagon;" our players are already there! A college player I tutored this past summer worked a high school baseball camp. It got his attention when he saw very few kids swinging "down" at the ball. Nevertheless, the instructors at the camp kept preaching the "down" swing to them, and kept praising them for their "good" swings—even when they weren't swinging down! There's something radically wrong with this picture. Do we teach what we really see? Do we even know what we are looking at?

A hitter must have an infinite number of swings—*all* within the context of his core mechanics—that enable him to counteract the varying planes of pitches that he must face during each at-bat. Why? Because, all pitches are not thrown to the same location or on the same elevation! Too many times, we instructors only teach one swing, e.g., "down," or "level." Hitters can get by with this in little league, but, what happens when hitters face sinkerball pitchers, or pitchers who can consistently throw strikes at the knees? I hear coaches and parents telling hitters to swing "level." *Have you ever tried to swing "level" at a pitch at your knees?* If you did, you probably wouldn't teach it; every kid isn't "Spiderman."

Good instruction all plays out smartly when one thinks of my definition of the "perfect" swing. *The 'perfect' swing is the adjustment the hitter makes to the pitch he gets*. We must teach mechanics that will help hitters make these on-the-fly adjustments. We owe it to them; we owe it to our programs.

The Advantages of Rotational Mechanics

Something I found out early-on in my study of hitting mechanics was that for every physical action, there must be an equal, opposite action. Because, no matter how much WE may *want* to "think" the skill of hitting is carried out, and how WE want it to be done, the fact of the matter is that—if it is to be done optimally, it MUST conform to the rules of biophysics and biomechanics. If it doesn't, the hitting sequences won't seamlessly mesh with each other. And if they don't, we see a robotic, unbalanced swing; certainly not one worthy of fluency—and ultimate production.

And, just what is "production?" Major league statisticians call production "O.P.S."—which is arrived at by ADDING TOGETHER a hitter's on-base percentage and his slugging percentage. In other words, O.P.S. is the ability for the player to "get on" (through hits and walks), PLUS his ability to drive in runs (high total bases). Obviously, a reason exists why the high OPS hitters bat third through sixth in your lineup? They produce runs—and runs win ball games.

I realize that EVERY player cannot have an OPS of 1.000 or more and hit clean-up. But, we can help those who may not possess the power and/or innate ability to achieve it. Rotational mechanics—and a smart hitting plan when going to the plate—have made up for many physical deficiencies over the years. The rotational swing not only provides the ideal physical properties needed for hitting success, it also provides the *leverage* to enhance a player's OPS.

The Hands

My mentor, Ted Williams, and I spent a glorious fall day back in the '80s discussing "hand position." "Where does a hitter gain the most leverage with his hands in the swing?" he would ask that day. Ted felt that more leverage was produced at the launch position with the hands *lower*, rather than higher. After hours of debate, the defining moment came when he rhetorically asked, "If you were going to punch someone, would you launch your punch from your ear—or your rib cage?" Our discussion abruptly ended right there. But, not before agreeing on two solid reasons for a low-hand position: 1) it was more conducive to a shorter, crisper swing, and 2) it resulted in increased leverage, thereby increasing bat speed and power.

Exactly where is the ideal "launch" area? Is there such a thing as a "universal" launch position for the hands? Williams used to say that a hitter's hands needn't be any higher than the uppermost area of the strike zone he must cover. However, some of us still teach hitters to keep their hands much higher—and swing down through the ball—and then wonder why some good-sized players show little power! There's very little leverage with the down swing.

Optimum placement of the hands at the vital launch position is a key, and moving them there during the pre-launch phase should be a "natural" movement for the hitter. WHERE a hitter positions his hands in the stance is a matter of his personal style. High, low, in, or out doesn't really matter, but he must feel comfortable, be tension-free, AND be able to get them into the proper launch position "on time." However, what is of importance here is *where* his hands move to as he strides and launches his swing. And, as you watch today's (and history's) elite, *productive* hitters, this area is in the region of the armpit. Some drop their hands to get to it, some raise their hands, some bring them back, and some move them forward. But, the swing is launched from the same area each time. However, it is NOT a 45° straight line from a hands-high position to contact.

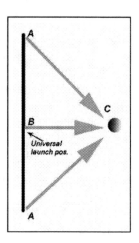

Look for it the next time you are watching a game on TV—and also watch the hitter's rear elbow "tuck in" as he approaches the launch position. If his elbow doesn't tuck in, a hitter cannot stay "inside" the ball. Correct pre-launch movements help break a hitter's inertia and also serve as a highly desirable "timing device" for him.

The Front Leg

In addition to the hands, a hitter can gain needed leverage through the proper use of his front leg. Now, you may be saying, what in the world does the FRONT leg have to do with the swing? The answer is more than most realize!

Many of you are aware of my comparison of the rotational swing with that of "winding a rubber band." In other words, our hands need a *propellant*, and this is furnished through "torque." Torque creates a "push-pull" effect on the hitter's body, resulting in increased energy.

The extent to which we can correctly increase this push-pull effect is directly proportional to the resulting velocity and the energy produced. The separation of the upper and lower torsos is identical for both hitters AND

From this position, Aaron Boone will bring his front knee rearward to a rigid position (at contact) as he lauches his swing.

Roger Clemens in classic torque position.

pitchers (for example, Aaron Boone and Roger Clemens). The lower half opens (begins rotating forward) as the upper half counter-rotates (rotates rearward). This creates "torque." Again, "winding the rubber band." Pretty simple. (even for us non-physics majors!).

A slingshot, in order to impart maximum velocity to a projectile, *must* be launched with a *rigid* wrist of the hand that is holding the slingshot. If our wrist is limp, a slingshot isn't very effective, if it would even work at all. And, neither will a baseball swing be productive with a "soft" front knee at contact. In physics, for every action, there is an equal and opposite action. In the slingshot example, as we *pull* the projectile back with one hand, we are *pushing* our other hand forward. In effect, "winding the rubber band."

We hear that pitching and hitting are "similar." Actually, the mechanics for both are *identical*, simply because they conform to the rules of biomechanics, as they must. *So, why is it that pitching coaches are basically on the "same page" teaching "technique," but hitting coaches teach mechanics that are sometimes 180° opposite from one another?* Does this make sense?

The next time you watch a ball game on TV, zero in on the hitter's front leg at CONTACT. Unless the hitter has been fooled by the pitch, his front leg will be RIGID. However, be advised to watch very, very closely; it lasts for a scant micro-instant, and then releases. *The rigid front leg is only needed at contact.*

Aaron Boone in correct leveraged position as he extends through contact. Note rigid front knee.

Photo credit: Otto Greule/Allsport

Photo credit: Matthew Stockman/Allsport

Note rigid front knees on both Ken Griffey, Jr. and Sean Green.

During the past generation, we have violated all these energizing principles of physics in hitting technique—we didn't need them. The ultra-high resiliency of aluminum bats made this possible. Today, the only way we can offset the less-resilient and heavier minus 3s is if we give the swing some type of "boost," or "enhancer." *The effect of the aluminum bat has acted in the past in the same way that the proper use of physics does on the baseball swing.*

To equalize the offset, we are now obliged to apply mechanics consistent with the laws of physics to overcome the lessened advantage of today's aluminum. *Leverage* counterbalances this significant loss.

Ok, Mike, But How Does It Happen?

In the swing, as the bat launches, the upper torso begins to come FORWARD to catch up to the already-rotating lower body. The front knee begins to simultaneously come BACK to provide the slingshot effect and leverage required to produce the desired high velocity. This counter-movement aids in the all-important *catapulting* of the hands forward. Without it, players are purely "hands-and-arms" hitters, normally incapable of producing the high bat velocity needed for an OPS consistent with the player's hitting type. "Effortless power versus powerless effort" is about the best way I know how to facilitate its understanding.

Once again, we see the push-pull effects in the good rotational swing. The hands move forward as the front leg comes back. In the final analysis, rotational hitting is a finely-honed *system of pulleys and levers* that effectuates the *equal and opposite* principle of maximizing kinetic energy.

Leverage is a very powerful tool! Good rotational mechanics, imparting optimum leverage, is a cornerstone of productive hitting. Use it effectively and reap the rewards.

CHAPTER 21

"The Important Role of Leverage: The Bats" (Part #2)

As a hitting instructor, I tell players that one of the many "gifts" I can give them is the ability to swing a longer, heavier bat—at approximately the same velocity—as the shorter, lighter bat they currently use. Contrary to mainstream thinking, this "gift" comes from a singular source—good hitting technique—not by lifting weights, taking "supplements" or "performance-enhancing" drugs. As you will hopefully see, "strength" can have less of an impact on hitting the ball hard than you might realize.

Leverage

Leverage is an assisted advantage. It was a Sicilian mathematician, Archimedes, who said, "Give me a lever long enough and a firm and immovable place to stand, and I will move the world." Such is the power of leverage! After all, folks, when we talk hitting technique, we're talking physics. And, *body leverage*, as well as *bat leverage*, are two crucial elements needed for optimal performance.

Okay. Assuming the size of the lever is *manageable*, the longer the lever, the greater the benefit received. Until the advent of the metal bat in the early 1970s, baseball's hitters had recognized and taken advantage of this physics phenomenon. They commonly referred to it as "whip."

Momentum

Hitting a baseball involves a transfer of momentum from the bat to the ball. Momentum is calculated as the product of *mass* times *velocity*. Simply, the greater the momentum—the greater the force of impact—the harder the ball will be hit. Furthermore, the greater the bat speed, the greater the force of impact. However, bat speed—by itself—has *little* impact on the swing without MASS.

Most everything in life involves a *compromise*, including hitting a baseball. We know a light bat can be swung faster. A heavier bat will impart more momentum to the ball; however, this is achieved normally at the expense of bat speed. A lighter bat will give the batter more control but less momentum. And, if you're using wood as the material, you can only reduce the weight so much. If the weight is reduced too much, the wood will be too soft, and/or the bat will be too small to hit the ball with authority.

The intrinsic characteristics of aluminum bats allow balls to be hit harder and farther than bats made of wood and provide hitters with decided advantages, particularly a rigid, light-weight material and ultra-high resiliency. But, it has also given many players a "false" sense of security, the belief that they could be an effective hitter—with either aluminum OR wood. In the majority of cases, history has proven otherwise. The player's technique more often than not becomes the determining factor. And, in exchange for the explosiveness of the aluminum bat came yet another compromise: hitters gave up their freedom of choice, as bat styles and selection became very limited.

Variety is the Spice of Life

Players come in all shapes and sizes. All have different personal "styles" and comfort levels that often require different bat models. I can still remember teammate and good friend Eddie Brinkman, a terrific shortstop with the Washington Senators. He had developed a reputation as a "good-field, no-hit" player over his long career. When Ted Williams became Washington's manager in 1969, he simply asked Eddie, "You're not a very big guy. Why do you always pull the ball?" In his own way, Ted "asked" him to change his hitting approach and hit according to his hitting "type." So, Eddie went 180° opposite and ordered heavy, very thick-handle bats, choked up about 3-4", used the whole field and raised his batting average 80 points. Eddie's *hitting* technique didn't change, but his hitting *approach* did. He aligned his body more closely to his axis of rotation to produce more line drives instead of harmless fly balls.

Frank Howard and I were asked to provide the power, and we responded to Williams' request by leading the American League in 1-2 home-run punch that year with 78. Our hitting approaches differed from Eddie's, because, physically, we were much bigger and stronger, and demanded more upslope from our swings. We did this by tilting back more on our axes. *The technique, however, was the same for all of us.*

If we were amateur players, with only aluminum bats at our disposal, we might not have found suitable bats to use. Somehow, I can't picture Big Frank, all 6'9" and 300 pounds of him, swinging a 34"-31 ounce "toothpick." Just thinking about that scenario makes me chuckle.

Before aluminum, there were an infinite number of bat sizes, weights, and lengths. You could always find a bat that felt "good"—long bats, short bats, thin handles, fat handles, no-knobs—in virtually any combination of weight, length and style. In most bat racks, you might not find two of the same model bat!

At the major league level, wood-bat manufacturers have always catered to the players' requests; they give them what they want. They had lathe templates back then and now use computer-aided design software for each bat model they wish to duplicate. Or, they can design a bat specifically for a particular player.

On the other hand, the intrinsic characteristics of aluminum are altogether different and preclude customization; the cost per bat would be prohibitive. So, in effect, amateur players are held "captive" by the bat manufacturers. Their molds mold us. Not so at the professional level.

Should One Size Fit All?

Because players don't have a big selection of aluminum bats to choose from, hitters over the past twenty five years have been *cloned*—they all *look* alike. They all *hit* alike. They all have the same stances and have used the same linear technique. And, they all pretty much swing the same model bat, notwithstanding the importance of the variances in their hitting "types" and physical sizes. Personally, I've never been able to find a *bottle-handle* aluminum bat, have you? And, I'll bet you know—or coach—a player or two like Eddie Brinkman who could really benefit from one. They aren't to be found. We must do it the "aluminum way" or not at all. I believe this can severely limit a hitter's upside.

I continually hear baseball people lament the fact that there is very little offensive strategy in baseball today. But, why should there be? One swing of the bat can produce four runs! Hitters aren't taught to hit behind the runners anymore, or move them along. Why play for ONE run? And, while there are coaches who would like to see more of this type of strategy in the game, the bats the players have at their disposal do not lend themselves to "pushing" the ball the other way (a la Brinkman). No one wants to be a "table setter." Everyone is down on the knob trying to be a hero—irrespective of size and strength. We tend to forget, however, that heroes come in many forms and sizes. *Every* player has an important place in the lineup. To be successful in this game, you've got to hit according to your hitting "type."

Over time, the aluminum-bat manufacturers kept reducing the various weights, lengths, and sizes of bats, so that everyone basically swung the "same" bat. Personal styles and technique were lost, as were the grand array of bat styles of wooden-bat days. This is not meant as an indictment against the bat manufacturers who have supplied excellent, state-of-the-art products to hitters over the years.

Does This Make Sense?

Now, think for a moment. Today's hitters are much bigger and stronger than when I played, and the pitchers don't throw nearly as hard. There were real "power" pitchers then, who took advantage of the higher mound, and threw much harder than today's sinker/slider-type pitchers. We regularly hit balls 400′, and a few to *over* 500′. I don't see today's hitters consistently approaching these distances. Yes, more home runs are being hit because of much smaller strike zones, harder baseballs, smaller parks, lower mounds, diluted pitching, and bigger players. When I played, there were only 24 teams; today, there are *30*. Before me, there were only *16*—and few other professional sports to play. Baseball had the pick of the talent pool of the country's best athletes every year. Relatively speaking, better athletes meant better competition, which yielded better pitching.

How were we able to use bigger bats, when we lacked the physical size and strength of today's hitters? None of us lifted weights; we needed jobs to support our families over the winter months. We didn't have the time to go to the gym; we needed to earn a living. I can truthfully tell you that some of the worst-looking bodies in the shower room belonged to yesterday's best hitters! No robotic, muscle-bound, chiseled bodies produced all those records. Did you know that, up until a few years ago, *42 of the top 50 home run hitters in major league history weighed LESS than 190 pounds?*

Many college players come to San Diego for hitting instruction. I smile when they tell me they are asked to "hit the weights hard over the summer. We need more power from you next year."

Before aluminum, the ability to use the *total* body within the parameters of biomechanics (NOT JUST THE HANDS AND ARMS) contributed largely to the fact that bigger bats could be used. What did this mean for the hitter? More *leverage*, more *whip* and more *momentum*. How hitters produce these factors is crucial to them hitting their potentials, because today's -3 aluminum bats lack the resiliency, weight, and length to generate the momentum needed to maximize it.

Why Linear Mechanics?

No one tried harder to understand the rationale behind linear mechanics than I did. As hard as I tried, I still could not understand the physics—or logic—behind a technique that promoted "lunging" and almost put baseball out of business at the turn of the twentieth century.

My conclusion was that linear mechanics worked ONLY because the ultra-light, highly-resilient aluminum bats and the lightning-quick Astroturf fields of that era could make up for a linear swing's mechanical inefficiencies. A hitter didn't have to have good mechanics or be blessed with great ability; all he needed was an aluminum bat. Ground balls through the infield on Astroturf produced doubles and triples, because fielders weren't quick enough to cut them off before they rolled past them to the fences. It is easy to see why and how ground balls and linear mechanics (hands/arm hitters) became so popular; the aluminum bat became the "Great Equalizer." Today, those advantaged offensive weapons are long gone. Yet, some of us still continue to teach those mechanics, to the detriment of the player.

Originally, the aluminum bat was simply a metal copy of a wood bat. They were more durable, so they were cheaper to use. But, it wasn't long before other advantages began to show up. Aluminum bats *could* be made much lighter and the barrels much bigger. And, because they are lighter, they could be swung faster than a wood bat. In addition, the hardness and resilience of aluminum resulted in considerably greater exit speeds ("trampoline effect") when the ball came off the bat.

Once the advantages of aluminum became apparent, the "race" was on. In an effort to increase a hitter's bat speed, more modern alloys and thinner "walls" were used, and the metal bat's weight-to-length ratio increased to an unbelievable -12! It's no wonder that *bat speed* became the buzzword. With aluminum, because its resiliency was so great, *weight* and *length* could be sacrificed. Hitters could hit the ball harder and further with shorter and lighter levers than ever before (defying both physics and Archimedes). This was certainly not possible with wood bats, and ushered in the era of "hands-and-arms," linear mechanics (back-to-front).

The "Changes"

Over time, the NCAA rules committee and the High School Baseball Federation rightly decreed that aluminum bats were dangerous and provided an unfair advantage to hitters. In 2000, the bat manufacturers were directed to alter their designs and make bats with a weight-to-length ratio not to exceed -3. Thus, the weight-to-length ratio had decreased over the years from -12s to today's mandated -3s. Statistical results for both high schools and colleges have decreased nearly 30% each year from the pre -3 days. *Same* players. Same mechanics. *Different* results. The only variable that changed was the metal bat's physical characteristics.

The Differences

Now, it may be said that a -3 is a -3, whether it be aluminum or wood. However, there remain two principal differences. One difference is the size of the "sweet spot" and the concept of being "jammed." With wood, the sweet spot is approximately 4 7/8" compared to an aluminum bat's approximate 16"-20". Getting jammed with wood breaks the bat and normally yields harmless contact; getting jammed with aluminum can still yield a hard-hit ball. With aluminum, the sweet spot is still pretty much the whole bat. Today, however, it's not nearly as "sweet" as the aforementioned statistics clearly show.

The other difference lies in a bat's *weight distribution*. As the weight-to-length decreased, the aluminum bat manufacturers, in an effort to keep their bats "light," put the increased weight inside the knob. The bat and effect is still a -3, but feels like a *lighter* -3. However, by doing this, the player loses the "whip effect" that he would experience with a wood bat, where much of the bat's weight is in the barrel, not the knob. The "feel" is altogether different. When you lose the weight in the barrel area and the associated whip, you lose momentum. And, momentum is the name of the game.

This difference can be demonstrated. Attach a six-pound medicine ball to a 2' length of rope. Pick up the medicine ball with the rope and begin twirling your body until the rope holding the bowling ball is parallel to the ground. As you are twirling, keep moving closer to a tree (or wall, if that is more convenient) and allow the medicine ball to hit the tree trunk. Feel the resulting concussion.

Next, attach a 10' length of rope to the same medicine ball. Begin twirling until the rope is parallel to the ground and repeat the previous steps. If done correctly, you will see that the longer rope will produce much more momentum (out where maximized *concussion* is sought).

This is the principle behind rotational mechanics. Kinetic energy begins with the feet, works upward through the legs and upper torso, and then out the shoulders and arms until ALL the energy is released at the end of the bat. Having a long lever increases this energy release! Hands-and-arms hitters do not experience this advantage.

Key point

Many players today use wood bats to practice with. I definitely recommend it, because it sends an accurate message back to the hitter when he *doesn't* hit the sweet spot. An aluminum bat gives little feedback, and this keeps the hitter from making good adjustments. You must remember that to get *similar* benefits from a wood bat, it *must* be slightly longer and heavier—and swung approximately at the same velocity as the metal bat you are currently using. In other words, if you swing a 33" aluminum bat, you'll need a 34" wood bat to offset the metal bat's inherent advantages. Likewise, with the bat's weight.

Although Babe Ruth used a very heavy bat (upwards of 42 ounces), players today use bats that weigh around 32 ounces, ostensibly to take full advantage of bat speed. While 32-ounce bats are certainly capable of providing enough momentum in the swing, many of these same players swing bats that are only 34 inches, depriving them of increased leverage, whip, and accelerated energy. LENGTH SHOULD BE AN IMPORTANT FACTOR IN CHOOSING A BAT, because leverage has a very positive effect on power and momentum.

All things being equal, a longer bat is capable of hitting a ball further. The action—and mechanical assist—of a longer lever provides much more power and force than a shorter one, and is a principal reason why wood bats MUST be longer. Wood, after all, does not have the high resiliency attributed to aluminum.

OK, Mike, What's the Remedy?

When a bat begins to feel "too" light in our hands, it sends a message to our brain: "you don't need to use your body!" With aluminum, we became a generation of "hands-and-arms" hitters, because our total body wasn't needed to generate power. My belief is that *bigger bats can cure many of the problems hitters embrace today*; they "force" the player to use his legs. And, as hitting continues to revert back to rotational mechanics, *we will continue to see hitters seeking longer and heavier bats*— PROVIDED THAT THE MECHANICS THEY USE ENABLE THEM TO APPROXIMATE THE BAT SPEEDS OF THE SHORTER, LIGHTER BATS. Rotational mechanics have been providing this benefit to players for over 100 years.

Today, an inordinate number of players I tutor are well over 6' 2" tall and weigh more than 215 pounds. They *need* longer and heavier bats, but can't find them. To my knowledge, the largest manufactured aluminum bat is 34". As the -3 aluminum bats become more like wood in size and resiliency, the aluminum-bat manufacturers will hopefully provide bigger bats to accommodate the diminished advantages of the -3s and also to satisfy the needs of today's considerably larger and stronger players.

Is a "Bigger" Bat for Everyone?

I'm not advocating that *everyone* should swing a heavier bat. I'm merely pointing out the power of "mindsets." We have been teaching and doing something altogether different for almost 30 years, and over time, it became *natural*. What I am suggesting is that, with good rotational mechanics, a hitter should *typically* be able to swing a longer, heavier bat *at near the same velocity* as he could with a shorter, lighter bat with a "hands-and-arms" approach. It is for this reason alone why we rarely see major league players who *don't* use rotational mechanics.

However, hitters should not make bat selection a "macho" decision, i.e., if a slightly heavier bat is good, a much heavier bat should be much better. Hitters should not fall into this trap! The bat a hitter uses must feel right and manageable, and still provide bat velocity consistent with optimizing momentum and solid contact.

In the past, aluminum bats made every hitter a threat, regardless of mechanics. It is now incumbent on the coach or player to make the proper changes to get the job done. As Ted used to say, "It ain't the arrow, it's the Indian." Aluminum reversed this thinking, becoming "It ain't the Indian, it's the arrow." Today, we're back to reality. The -3s dictate it.

It's Not About "Theory"

Like most individuals, I learned hitting mechanics through emulation, watching and copying hitters when I was growing up. When I later played in the major leagues, the emulation phenomenon didn't slow down, but accelerated. I was like "a kid in a candy store." What I teach today, I used, experienced, and saw *first-hand*. Up close and personal. I didn't learn physics first and subsequently apply it to hitting later. I saw *what* worked and *why* it worked. What I try to bring to these articles is this firing-line *experience*, not "theory." Too many of us try to teach theory, when we should be asking *what works?* What am I *really* seeing here? Good information means absolutely nothing if we can't communicate it vocally, through the written word, demonstrably, or graphically in a way that the coach or player can understand and use effectively.

I have indeed been fortunate to have experienced this rare opportunity to study hitters at baseball's highest level. After a while, it became clear why so many players used rotational hitting and why it has worked for more players over a longer period of time than any other technique. In fact, 95% of baseball's Hall of Fame hitters used this very same technique. I feel privileged so many have shared their good information with me over the years.

However, nothing in life is constant—except change. I don't know everything there is to know about hitting and continually ask questions, with the hope that I may learn a BETTER way of teaching and be smart enough to pass it on for everyone to improve. My approach is not to tell players or coaches that this is the ONLY way to hit. Rather, it is by getting you to ask questions: Is this logical? Does it make sense? If I can get you to do this, I feel I have succeeded. *Which* technique you ultimately decide to use is your decision. We should have a choice; unfortunately, when it comes to hitting, we usually don't.

It's All About Hitting the Ball Harder

Will this article automatically make a hitter better? Of course not; there are many other variables to consider if one is to take advantage of the items I've reviewed in this article. There's a place for every hitting "type" in baseball (as Eddie Brinkman found out). Singles/contact, line-drive/gap, and pure power-type hitters can ALL benefit from increased momentum and leverage. We're not talking home runs here, we're talking about hitting the ball HARDER, which has advantages for ALL hitting types. Learning rotational mechanics correctly can enhance leverage and momentum in the swing, and should be on every motivated hitter and coach's agenda. Why make a tough task such as hitting—even *tougher?*

CHAPTER 22

"How to Hit Productively with the Minus 3 Bats"

My telephone wouldn't stop ringing after last summer's all-star game. Concerned parents saying, "I didn't see one player on this year's all-star team batting like my son is being taught." And confused players saying, "I didn't see anyone 'squishing the bug,' or 'watching the ball hit the bat,' or 'swinging down at the ball,' or 'hitting on their front foot,' like my coach tells me to do. What gives?"

What exactly is it about mechanics that confuses us so that we can't even "see" the mechanics of the players who grab all the headlines and make all the money? When parents and players are asking questions like the aforementioned ones, we coaches have a problem. WE should be telling THEM about the changes going on. We should be on the leading edge, teaching leading-edge mechanics. But, this isn't happening. Is it because we don't know what to look for? Is it because we teach what we hear? Or read? Or teach what we were taught when we were playing? Is it because of today's proliferation of instant information—both good and bad—that's made hitting so confusing?

The "Grim Reaper"

Both players and coaches have to solve this dilemma, because the advent of the "Grim Reaper"—better known as the −3 aluminum bat—is now upon us. Last year, the N.C.A.A. mandated that the −3s are to be used by all collegiate baseball teams. And, when the results were tallied up at the end of last season, overall hitting production, including batting averages, was down over 25%! That's an inordinate number, considering the only variable in the equation that had changed was the bat standard. This year, as everyone is well aware, high schools must use these -3s, too. If this caused such a problem with the more mature college players, what will be the results with the younger, less experienced players? And, you might ask, how could such a measly two-ounce change produce such disproportionate results? Let's look at history to help provide the answer.

Oh, Baby! Minus 12s! I was already in the big leagues when the aluminum bats made their debut in the early 1970s. Up until that time, all bats in collegiate baseball were wood. To be successful with wood bats, the hitter had to use his *entire* body to hit. Bats, in those days, were much longer and heavier than they are today. I remember swinging a 35"/34 ounce bat at the University of California (Berkeley) for four years. Today, we would call this a "minus 1." Later on, professionally, I swung a 35" bat, with weights varying from 33-35 ounces. A "log" by today's standards. But, I wasn't alone. There were players swinging heavier and longer bats than I was. Because, we could. Because, we used our legs effectively to hit, and we rotated. We had to, or we didn't get very far. If wood bats were too "light," the wood was invariably too soft to be effective.

If my memory serves me, when the aluminum bats were introduced, they were minus 12s. Now, think about this for a moment. With a bat that light, all a player had to do was stand at home plate and "flick" his wrists and hit the ball 430'. And they did. *When the aluminum bat came in, productive hitting mechanics basically went out.* A player didn't really "need" mechanics—he just needed to swing. The biggest mistake hitters made using these bats was, simply, taking pitches. "Don't get cheated" became the buzzword. We instantly became "20 second hitters." Plate discipline went out the door. On the other hand, with wood bats, a player had to be selective and dead-on, *every time*, to be productive. Overnight, we became a sport of hands-and-arms hitters. We didn't need our legs to hit. We just needed them to get us to the batters' box.

Astroturf was also beginning to make its mark on professional baseball at this time, followed by many colleges and universities. Remember those days of pinball baseball in the National League? Faded fields of artificial turf with huge watermarks and stains and permanent yard markers left over from NFL games? New multi-use stadiums were being built that incorporated this new, ultra modern "carpet." To take advantage of these "fast" playing fields, offensive baseball went through another metamorphosis. "Little" ball—"rabbits" running rampant on artificial turf in Cincinnati, Pittsburgh, St. Louis, Houston, Philadelphia and Montréal were in vogue. Keeping the ball on the ground became the rule of the day.

College and high school coaches and amateur players, as per custom, "copied" their professional brethren in terms of game strategy and accompanying hitting mechanics. Scouts turned their "attention" to signing players who could "fly." Many a player was drafted with these qualifications: "A great athlete. Can really run. Limited experience. Must teach him to hit." Teaching him to hit was to teach him to put the ball in play—on the ground, and run like hell. Astroturf infields were so fast, infielders couldn't catch up to the ground balls. We were taught to swing down and let our weight come on to the front side to facilitate the down swing. This went on for about twenty years.

Accordingly, we entered baseball's "Jack Rabbit Era." *Hands-and-arms hitters, speed, contact, ground balls,* and *"little ball"* then became the new buzzwords. *Pulling the ball, fly balls,* and *home runs* were out. A terrific club, managed by a wonderful manager, Whitey Herzog (a former manager of mine), the world champion St. Louis Cardinals of the mid '80s epitomized this trend.

Today, it's a new era. Only Montréal and Philadelphia in the NL still have plastic grass, and many colleges and universities have reverted back to natural grass. Astroturf, diving (to cover the outside corner), *getting the weight to the front side* ("lunging"), and *swinging down,* are dinosaurs of the past. We're in a "new-old" age of hitting now. We've gone back to pre-aluminum bat mechanics, back to the days of baseball's Golden Era (1920-1970), and the upsurge in hitting and offense at the major-league level has been overwhelming.

❏ *Minus 3s or wood. What's the difference?* This hitting change began about 1995— all over *again*! Astroturf had been phased out and aluminum bats had gone from −12s to −5s. Too many players were complaining about "making contact," but were getting jammed all the time, and having little power. "Powerless effort" as opposed to the desired "effortless power." My feeling, at that time, was this was happening, because players were still using the same mechanics that were taught when the −12s first came out. But, with −5s, you needed more than just your arms and hands to hit with. You needed your legs, too. I can go to any ML bat rack and pull out −3 wood bats. Nice, straight grain, dense wood. Lots of big leaguers use −3s. 35/32s, 34/31s, *et al.* No problem. So, today, what's the difference between wood and aluminum? Not much. A −3 is a −3. And, that's the heart of this article.

How Do We Solve This Problem?

Well, first of all, we have to recognize the problem. And, as coaches and instructors, I don't believe we've done a very good job of this. We keep teaching what WE were taught when WE played, when aluminum bats were much lighter. I guess this is normal; we teach what we know best. But, we also must acknowledge that *the only constant in life is change,* and, over time, this inevitability becomes reality. Most of us find change distasteful, and resist it, or turn our backs to it. "Maybe if I don't acknowledge it, it'll go away." The inevitability is this won't happen. The change has been in progress for over five years now. The hitting approach has changed. But, we haven't. Parents notice it. Players see it. But, we instructors/coaches don't—or don't want to. Yet, we owe it to our players. They look to us for help and guidance getting them to the "next" level and hitting their potentials.

To fix the problem, we have to learn how to rotate and correctly get the lower body into the swing. I have given one-on-one instruction to over 2,300 players in nearly twenty years. This total doesn't include seminars, clinics, or teams—just "one-on-one" instruction. And, of this total, incredibly, not ONE player who has come to me for instruction was using his lower half *correctly* in the swing. Not one! Many players profess to, and think they are. I ask players all the time. "Why don't you use your lower body?" And they respond by saying, "I thought I was. My coach says for us to get more "hips" into the ball, but I'm not sure he really knows, because he doesn't tell us how." Well, if a player is only using "half" his body, he might as well go up to the plate with "half" a bat. (Interesting, but no player to whom I've said this, has replied that's a "good" idea; no one wants to hit with a 16-17" bat!) Yet, day after day, game after game, they try to "roll boulders uphill." And, they wind up leaving baseball pre-maturely because they have no fun. I've never known a player who hit .150 that had fun.

So, think about this: the absolutely *strongest* muscles in our bodies, the legs, don't even get used! Why not? Because the light aluminum bats have put us to sleep. We didn't need the legs to hit before. We do now.

"I Really Thought I Had a Chance. I Just Couldn't Hit With a Wood Bat"

I see terrific players I've known here in San Diego all the time. I saw one last May and asked him what he was doing home. He said he got released. I mean, this kid could hit. He told me he just couldn't hit with a wood bat. I'm sure this is regrettably repeated far too many times each year. This kid was a high draft choice with good size. He had NO power with wood. I asked him what he was being taught in the minor leagues. You guessed it. What a waste. Today, unless we get smarter and open our eyes to what's really happening, there's going to be a lot more unhappy hitters (and coaches) looking for answers.

To Teach Correctly, We Shouldn't Teach Just "Parts"

After being selected the Topps™ and *Sporting News*™ minor league "Player of The Year" in 1966, I went to spring training with the Baltimore Orioles the following spring. After hitting a number of long batting practice home runs one day, Frank Robinson, the AL's MVP the previous year, said to me, "Rook, you've got big-time power. But, you're gonna find—with the better pitchin' up here—that you're gonna have to 'fight' for good pitches to hit. And, you'll find that you'll get better pitches if you move closer to the plate." Wow! That made sense. And, why wouldn't I take the advice of a great hitter like F. Robby? Even now, as I write this, I remember playing on two different teams with him (Orioles and Angels), and consider him the best hitter I ever played with.

The next day, I moved closer to the plate, from 16" to 12". And, Robby was right! I DID get better pitches to hit. I just couldn't do anything with them! I shattered 15 bats in seven games. The pitchers jammed me so bad, my top hand was black and blue for three months.

When we give advice to hitters, many times we only give "bits" and "pieces" of it. When I moved closer to the plate, I also needed to adjust my swing and body positioning to compensate for this spatial change. To be close to the plate, your hands absolutely have to stay "inside the ball," or you're going to get jammed. If you're casting your hands out over the plate, offsetting your sweet spot further out from you, you're also moving the handle of the bat closer to where your sweet spot *was*. To cover the pitch away, in my rookie days, I strode somewhat "toward" the plate, closing down my hips in the stride. This made me somewhat vulnerable to the pitch "in," but minor league pitchers couldn't "thread the needle" like the big leaguers could. So, I got lulled to sleep with my success.

After moving closer, I continued doing the same things as before, striding towards the plate, because I didn't know any better—and nobody told me anything different. After one week, I was back off the plate, giving the good ML pitchers more room to "operate" on me. And operate, they did!

The point in this regard is every time you make an adjustment to your swing, no matter how slight, it impacts other parts of your body. I had a 16-year old player and his dad call me for an evaluation a couple of weeks ago. I asked him why he felt he needed private instruction. His dad told me that he had lost his ability to "drive" the ball. I asked the player what he was being taught. He said his coach is telling everyone to "stay back." I said "OK." Anything else? He said, "No," that everything else was still the same. I asked him how it felt to do this. He asked, "Why?" I asked him if his coach teaches "level shoulders." He said, "Oh, yes. He's "big" on that." I asked him to take a few dry swings for me, emphasizing keeping his weight over his back leg and absolutely resist coming forward—while swinging down (level shoulders). He tried to do this, but said it didn't feel right.

The reason it didn't feel right is because his body was going in *opposite* directions. When you swing with level shoulders, the path of your swing is down; your weight naturally comes forward. What he was being asked to do was not natural. Part of his body was being asked to stay back, while the other part was asked to come forward. Accordingly we have to be very careful what we tell hitters so that we don't confuse them. If we want a player to stay back, we must also have him make some other body and swing adjustments to complement it. He must also "sit down over his back leg," and dip his rear shoulder on his approach. Doing so will allow his back elbow to tuck in and his lead elbow to naturally work up. This will get him on the right track to match the plane of his swing to the plane of the pitch. We should try to teach a "system," rather than bits and pieces. Contrary to some individuals, my experience is the parts of different systems don't mix.

Why Are "THEY" Doing This (Minus 3s) to Us?

Actually, "they" are not doing this TO you; actually, "they" are doing it FOR you! The −3 rule was actually put into effect to counteract the potential for serious injury and the extraordinarily high "exit speeds" of batted balls. Thank goodness for that! But, in reality, this ruling will also do more for good, solid, hitting mechanics than anything since the advent of the aluminum bat. The players must learn the mechanics and make the adjustments necessary to hit their potentials. In the long run, it will not only make it easier for the amateur player, but also for the would-be professional as he transitions to the wood bat. If he's learned rotational and lower body mechanics correctly, he won't miss a beat. The swing mechanics *should* be identical. After all, physics is physics.

What About the Bat Manufacturers?

We players always blame our bats, then pick up and use the bats of the "hot" hitters on the team, thinking this will make the "difference." Williams used to tell me, "Mike, it ain't the arrow, it's the Indian." Not very "politically correct" by today's standards, but it makes its point! Good mechanics go a long way in helping a player hit his potential.

Did you ever take time to think that a baseball bat is about the only retail product you can buy today that comes with NO directions concerning how to use it? Could you imagine your computer without a "help" menu? Or installing an engine cam shaft without directions? Or putting up "track" lighting? I mean, bat manufacturers sell bats, pure and simple. They take no responsibility for their use or whether you're successful. They only give us what we want. And, over the past 25 years, they have given us the light bats that our hitting mechanics craved. Have you ever noticed the "scalloped" out ends of wood bats? Sure you have. As players came up from the minor leagues, they requested light bats. They grew up on aluminum. But, as wood bats became shorter and lighter in weight, the wood also became less dense and much softer. To get better wood, the bat manufacturers used wood that would ordinarily go into bats weighing a few ounces more, then would reduce the weight of the bat by hollowing out the end. The trend, today, is for longer, heavier bats. We are seeing less scalloped ends. We shouldn't blame the bat manufacturers; they only give us what we ask for.

As more and more players transition into rotational mechanics, the bat manufacturers should see more orders for these longer and heavier bats. Since the aluminum bats came on the scene, the trend has been for lighter and shorter bats because of the dominance of the hands and arms in the swing. For years, a player couldn't find a 35" bat. Utilizing the legs correctly, players will naturally gravitate to bigger bats. The bats they're using today will feel too light; they won't feel very comfortable. And, with the lighter bat, the *hitter will try to use his hands more than he should*. His focus will be on the hands, instead of letting the big muscles of his legs pull the small muscles of his hands and arms through.

Why Can't I Swing a Heavier Bat?

When I played, there were an infinite number of different bat styles, weights, and configurations. More than I could count. Over the years, there have been very few aluminum bat models to choose from. Players 6'5" and 5'8" are swinging the same bats! Today, this condition remains, and in a minor-league bat rack, you'll *maybe* see three or four different bat styles. And, all will be 33-34 1/2" and 30-31 ounces. Over the past twenty five years, we've done a "thorough" job of "cloning" hitters; there is no need for choice. We all look the same—and swing the same—all predicated on the –5 and lighter aluminum bats. We need to allow for the individual "styles" of each hitter. They're *all* different.

Players today are much *bigger* and *stronger* than at any other time in the sport's history. Combine that with better physical conditioning, weight training, and the super "supplements" that players take to enhance their conditioning, and, well, suffice to say, these guys are pretty strong. MUCH stronger than their counterparts a generation earlier. Why, then, have the bats gotten *shorter* and *lighter*? We know bat speed alone is not the common denominator for power. Momentum is. "Momentum" in the swing is a product of the bat's MASS times velocity.

A few short years ago, everyone was teaching that bat speed as an end in itself—the most important part of the swing—the *ultimate* goal. I agree that bat speed IS important, but not at the expense of mass! A simple example: could a player hit a ball further if he swung a 35"-33 ounce bat at 85 mph, or if he used a 25"-15 ounce bat at 95 mph? Or 100 mph? We NEED leverage and weight—along with the velocity. The idea here is to get the big muscles to do the work, not just the hands and arms. By doing so, the player will still maintain the high bat speed but also get the weight and leverage needed to drive the ball and be productive.

Previously, I discussed the three "core" mechanical movements of 95% of baseball's Hall of Fame hitters. The answer to this question, "why can't I swing a heavier bat?" lies in those articles. I urge you to re-read them with this question in mind. The answer will "jump" out at you. We CAN swing bigger bats. We just need to learn the right mechanics.

But, one thing we should remember, that we learned in a previous article—the hands must stay "inside the ball." They must stay relatively close during the swing. In an earlier article, I talked about "leverage" with the longer bat, but we also know the principles of leverage work to the hitter's advantage, if he keeps his hands and bat close to his body in the swing.

We can demonstrate this by having the player hold a heavier object, like a rock or a dumbbell. The player can easily support this heavier weight if he holds it close to his body. Now, if he extends the object out away from him, maintaining the same height, he's really got to strain to hold it. It requires much greater effort on his part. The same principle holds true in the swing. If a player pre-extends (hits around the ball), he's going to pay the ultimate price—lower bat speed, a lighter bat, and a subsequent loss in momentum.

"THEY" are doing everyone a favor. We need to be smart enough to take advantage of it!

OK, Mike, You've Convinced Me. What's the Next Step?

First of all, I didn't invent these mechanics. When I write these articles, I am "standing on the shoulders" of an enormous number of talented players, past and present. I've asked questions. Lots of 'em. Too many of them, I suppose. Joe DiMaggio once told me I was wasting my time looking for the answers. "Either you were born with it, or you weren't," he would laugh and tell me. I've thought about that many times.

I guess I'm luckier than most. I know a lot of these players, past and present, having played the game at the ML level. These players knew a lot of the old timers—who also knew players from the 'teens and '20s. They've been kind enough to share their good information with me. Then, there's the longstanding mentor relationship I've had with the "world's greatest hitter," Ted Williams. Ted gave me some great advice over thirty years ago. "If you want to be a great hitter, study the moves of the great hitters. They're great for a reason." I did. Joe DiMaggio did, too, whether he wanted to admit it or not. We all do. Emulation is a powerful teacher. Some have the ability to do it; most can't.

For those who can't, we instructors need to be there to put them in these advantaged positions through proper instruction. Every "body" needs a blueprint for success. This is the reason I have come out with my videotape, "Do We Teach What We Really See?" It is more than just the baseless "sit and spin" and "stay back" and "drive your back knee to the ball" mechanics being taught by some individuals who realize a change in hitting is going on, but don't fully understand the *total* system. Far from it. By following the verbal and visual directions on my videotape, *anyone* can teach these mechanics the "right" way. You can see it unfold visually as the demonstrating players put it "all" together for us.

I know how good I feel when my students tell me that they can see "their" new mechanics being used by the big leaguers. Being able to see this has a huge positive impact on their self-images and confidence levels. They know they're on the right track, which—in turn—translates very positively to their on-the-field performance. They are hitting the ball further and harder than ever before. Confidence represents a huge part of hitting success.

Again, I didn't concoct any of this. These mechanics have been used for nearly 100 years, and its proponents account for 95% of baseball's Hall of Fame hitters. Not 25 year-old fads brought on by aluminum bats and Astroturf. One hundred years of solid history, with seemingly no end in sight. We're entering that era all over again with the minus 3s. Shouldn't we *all* be "on board?"

CHAPTER 23

"Regaining the 'Balance Point'"

A number of years ago, major league baseball had a terrific young hitter named Phil Plantier. By 24, he already had a 34-home run campaign and was staking his claim as baseball's next superstar. Unfortunately, Phil faded quickly after that, and by the time he was 28, he was out of the game. What happened? How could such a promising career get derailed so quickly?

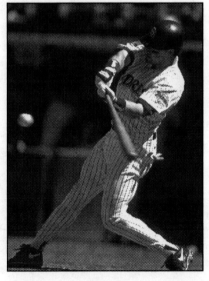

Photo Credit: Al Bellow/Allsport

Phil Plantier "collapsed" his back leg too much which produced a "too-steep" swing gradient which prematurely ended his promising ML career.

When you studied Phil's swing, you noticed a very steep swing gradient. This made it very difficult for him to catch up to high fastballs. My mentor, Ted Williams, used to say the high fastball was the most difficult pitch to hit because you had less time to react to that pitch than any of the others. This proved true in Phil's case and precipitated his rapid decline. His inability to make the proper mechanical adjustments to the high pitch ultimately proved fatal. Sadly, it could have been easily corrected.

Now, I can't tell you why Phil didn't, wouldn't, or couldn't make the proper adjustment(s). I remember Bruce Bochy, the San Diego Padres' manager asking me back in 1997 what I thought it would it take to fix him. We both saw his over-exaggerated uppercut and felt that this was holding him back. Boch wanted him fixed; he needed his bat in the lineup.

What You See Isn't Always What You Get!

Most people would tell a hitter displaying those symptoms to "level off" his swing more. And, that would be good advice. In actuality, Phil had a nice, powerful swing, displaying two of the three core mechanical movements of the proper rotational swing: his hips led his hands and he stayed inside the ball well. On the other hand, his swing gradient proved "inflexible;" he had difficulty "matching the plane of his swing to the plane of the pitch." He swung "up" at *every* pitch, regardless of location.

You've heard me say that swinging "up" too much is just as bad as swinging "down" too much, and that my definition of the *perfect swing* "is the ability of the hitter to adjust to the pitch he gets." So, while Boch told me his hitting people were focusing on his swing gradient, I casually mentioned to him that I didn't think that was the fundamental problem. "You *don't?*" he said, almost incredulously.

When correcting hitters, we must continue tracing back, sequence by sequence, until we spot the one deviation that *leads* to the swing break-down. It's *always* there to be found; we just have to be smart enough—or have enough experience—to know what to look for. Analyzing Phil's swing showed this breakdown occurring in his STRIDE, *not* his swing! So, let's analyze this important part of the player's swing.

The Stride

Hitters stride for a variety of reasons, most notably to break inertia, to set up an axis of rotation (AOR), and to re-establish the balance point in their swing.

Breaking inertia is the hitter's way of "getting started." It is very difficult for a hitter to hit from a stand-still position. For *aesthetic* reasons, I prefer my hitters to demonstrate a "quiet" approach. But, reality dictates that a good hitting instructor should not force his players' styles—unless they are incapable of getting to the "universal" launch position *on time*. So, I normally don't tutor this element of the swing. Hitters must feel comfortable with their own particular styles, but they STILL must break inertia in enough time to get to a good hitting position.

For the same reason pitchers use a *windup*, preliminary movement also gives the hitter a "head start" for the task-at-hand. I don't remember seeing many successful hitters in the major leagues that didn't move rhythmically BEFORE pitch release.

There are other ways to describe breaking inertia, including "rhythm," "dancing with the pitcher," and "turn your back to the pitcher when he turns his back to you." No matter how it is conveyed to the hitter, he must understand the cornerstone role that "getting started" plays in the good swing.

The hitter must also set up an axis of rotation (AOR) in his stride. The AOR provides an imaginary "pole" around which his body will rotate. Once the hitter strides and sets up his AOR, when his front heel drops, his head does not move forward as he rotates around his axis. If it does, he is *drifting*.

Loading Up

Re-establishing the balance point is a vital and integral component of the correct swing. A common coaching cue used today is "load up." This is in vogue, because we are trying to get our players to "stay back"—not "come forward"—which was yesterday's buzzword. I find that if the player is taught to load up in his stance, and doesn't regain the balance point in his stride with the proper weight-shift—or doesn't dip his rear shoulder on his swing approach—the amount of weight he holds on his back side will flow in an equal amount to his front side as he swings. This will sustain the drifting (lunging) condition. Or, equally as bad (as in Plantier's case), he will not weight-shift correctly (or at all) to his balance point and subsequently *collapse* his back side, yielding a too-steep gradient to his swing.

Balance means 50-50. For the player not to lunge—or collapse his back side—he MUST re-gain the balance point in his stride, and MAINTAIN IT *until* he launches his swing. In short, "loading up" is an acceptable cue *as long as the hitter regains the balance point when he strides.*

Stride Length

I have found that the distance between a player's feet, in his stance, should be equal—or close—to the length of his bat. A hitter will normally seek his natural balance point, just as you or I, in our daily activities. For anyone to be "off" balance is to be uncomfortable. If a player's normal walking stride is 33", and the distance between his feet in his stance is, say, 18", then he'll stride to his natural balance point of 33". His stride will be the difference between these numbers, or 15". So, if you put a hitter's feet at 33" to start, he most likely won't feel the "need" to stride further. At that point, have the player simply turn his foot out to a 45° angle, landing with his front heel OFF the ground. Putting him in this position will minimize (or eliminate) his stride

and allow him to work his rear leg closer to the ground. It's near impossible to keep your rear thigh perpendicular to the ground from an extreme upright position. Get him to widen his stance, and see if that doesn't help him!

Whether a hitter has an extremely wide—or extremely narrow—stance makes no difference; they will STILL seek their balance point (comfort zone). Jeff Bagwell of the Houston Astros is a good example. He starts out TOO wide, then strides *backward* to get to his proper balance point. Doing so helps him break inertia and also acts as an effective "timing device." Color commentators are "amazed" that he does this, but when you know the reason *why* hitters do this, it makes a lot of sense! No coach can tell a player what his comfort position should be. It is different for everyone, so be careful when coaching a hitter's style.

Photo Credit: Jed Jacobson/Allsport

Balance. Balance. Balance

OK. The player must re-gain the balance point in the stride. In addition to a hitter's balance point controlling the swing gradient, without proper preparation (balance), the dynamic sequencing of the torque loses its significance. It is virtually impossible to rotate the hips optimally using only "one" leg. Proper rotation requires both legs balanced to ensure maximum rotational velocity. Many times, you will see a major league hitter holding weight on his back side (loading up) in his stance, but when he strides, he re-gains the balance point. Again, if the player doesn't (transfer his weight correctly), two things happen: he will collapse his back side, creating a swing gradient much too steep for the plane of the pitch, or he will displace an equal amount of weight forward onto his front side in the approach phase, causing his body to lunge.

In the proprietary drills that I show on my videotape set (*Do We Teach What We Really See?*) to keep this from happening, I advocate getting a little bit more weight FORWARD in the stride, because when the front heel drops, the rear shoulder begins to dip. And, as the rear shoulder dips, it "allows" the lead elbow to start working slightly upward. As this happens, the player's weight AUTOMATICALLY shifts back to the inside of the rear thigh; his forward movement is "blocked," and the momentum revolves (rotates) around the axis. Try it! When people ask me how to stop a player from lunging, this is what I show them. It works!

Phil Plantier's problem was his weight never transferred to the balance point; it all stayed back. Then, when he dipped his rear shoulder in the approach, his back side "collapsed," causing a too-steep gradient to his swing. When I saw him play a year or two later, his swing was equally bad. They over-corrected and had him swinging straight down through the ball. Unfortunately, swinging down leveled his shoulders and made his weight come forward, and made him lunge. He was out of baseball the next year.

Hitting Position

Baseball people always talk about getting into a "good hitting position." But, what is a good hitting position? Hitting technique parallels "Murphy's Law" to the letter, in that "if you start off bad, things will continue to go bad." So, getting to a "good hitting position" should be Step Number One. This makes a lot of sense.

Otto Greule/Allsport

My definition of the proper hitting position occurs AFTER the hitter has taken his stride. He is balanced (or weight slightly on his *front* side), his upper body is counter-rotating (going back), his hips have begun to open and his front heel is off the ground. From this advantaged position, the hitter has *everything* going for him.

All he has to do is drop his front heel, and everything flows correctly. But, to make *this* happen correctly, the hitter must re-gain the balance point in his stride.

Jeff Kent in the "perfect" hitting position.

Today's Popular Cue

Today, once again, *lunging* is considered a bad word. "Staying back" is the buzzword. Yet the same coaches who teach staying back also teach level shoulders, keep the barrel of the bat above the hands, keep the rear shoulder up, etc. I don't say these cues are right or wrong, since everyone is entitled to their opinion. But, lunging, in *my* opinion, is not where a hitter's potential lies.

Lunging will dissipate bat speed and power in the swing as fast as anything I know of! Just this afternoon, I had a lesson with a player who told me what his coach was telling him. He told me he wanted his players to swing level-to-down and keep their weight back. Okay, here's where the problems and confusion set in with hitters. Ever try to stay BACK and swing DOWN—or level—at the same time? Try it. So, hitters today are confused because their bodies are being torn in opposite directions.

In our haste to teach the new buzzwords, we forget that other variables must also change. In effect, there are only TWO hitting systems: linear and rotational. Each system

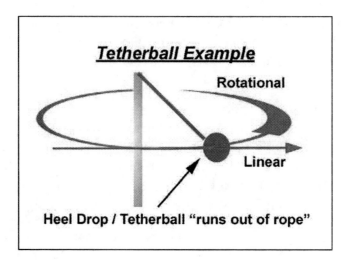

Tetherball Example

Rotational

Linear

Heel Drop / Tetherball "runs out of rope"

has its own set of "laws" that govern its physical movements. In most instances, they should not be combined!

However, one "shared" movement is the *weight transfer*. In linear hitting, the weight begins coming forward in the stride and *continues* coming forward through contact and the follow-through. In other words, the hitter's weight is one continuous movement towards the oncoming pitch.

In rotational hitting, there is also a weight transfer forward in the stride, but once the front heel drops to trigger the swing, the front side is *blocked*, and the hitter's linear movement becomes rotational. One must remember that when the front foot plants, it blocks the front side and the linear movement initiated in the stride. Body momentum at this point revolves around the axis, precluding lunging—much like the tether ball example I use in my videotape.

My goal in this instance is to simplify this movement for you in a way that you can easily understand and teach (or use). In the tetherball diagram, if we throw a tetherball as hard as we can, it passes the pole to which it is tethered. When the tetherball "runs out of rope," it violently rotates around the pole to which it is attached. Thus, we can graphically see the transition from linear to rotational. Dropping the front heel is ONE of the keys for blocking the weight transfer. This movement can be compared to the tetherball when it "runs out of rope." Both turn linear movement into rotational energy.

Today, we tell hitters to "stay back," ostensibly because—whether we realize it or not, we are making an attempt to teach rotational hitting! I don't know why this is, but coaches will try to teach concepts which they are not totally familiar with, simply because there is a new buzzword, e.g., "stay back." We must have command of our knowledge if we are to communicate effectively.

Photo credit: Jed Jacobson/Getty Images

Barry Bonds in the torque position. Notice his perfect balance.

The Remedy

Rotational hitters "sit down" as they swing, perpetuating the (inverted) "L-shaped angle" of the rear leg. Hitters MUST be taught to re-establish the balance point in their stride. By doing this, it keeps the swing gradient "natural" as the rear shoulder dips. If a player holds the greater percentage of his weight on the backside during the stride, he has a very good chance of "collapsing" his backside and will swing up too much.

As we see players transitioning from linear to rotational mechanics over the past few years, we see a large number of them exaggerate holding weight on their backside. This is normally the result of not having learned rotational mechanics correctly. For the player not to lunge, he MUST re-gain the balance point in his stride, and maintain it when he launches his swing. However, *"loading up" is acceptable as long as the hitter regains the balance point when he strides.*

CHAPTER 24

"What is a Quality AB?"

The Anaheim Angels' hitting in the 2002 World Series has re-kindled interest in such oft-used terms as "team hitting," "situational hitting," "deep counts," *et al*. The Angels exhibited a remarkable maturity in their approach to the game. Deep counts and foul balls, prolonged plate appearances—all fashioned until the pitcher made a mistake. This was what Scott Spiezio did in his crucial at-bat that triggered game 6's comeback, the one that ended with his three-run homer.

As a hitting instructor, I read and hear it all the time. "We're looking for our hitters to have quality at-bats." We all talk about it, but it seems many of us just use the expression without delving into a deeper meaning to communicate the concept to our players.

Communication can come in the way of making the players aware of your commitment to this offensive strategy by daily reminders. Professionally, it can be done through fines (e.g., kangaroo court). But, I've found the best way to get it done is by peer pressure, whereby the players themselves routinely have contests and keep score of this efficiency. Purely and simply, what has spurred the concept of "getting deep in the count" is the postage-sized strike zones of major league umpires. These small strike zones enable hitters to constantly be ahead in the count, and able to anticipate predictable pitches in predictable count situations. It is arguably the most important reason for baseball's increased slugging over the past few years. In fact, one of the most important functions of a hitting coach is to KNOW who is behind the plate that day. Knowing whether he is a hitters' or pitchers' umpire *can* go a long way in determining your hitting strategy that day.

Hitting statistics don't lie. Given enough at-bats, hitters provide a trend that ultimately tells the true story of their production and efficiency. To snap out of an offensive funk, hitters often need to string together more quality at-bats, by simply putting the ball in play and not striking out.

In order to implement an offensive strategy, a coach must have a guideline. My quality-at-bat criteria are measured by how well a batter manages the strike zone, and his ability to *time* pitches. When a hitter does these two things well, he will normally produce a quality at-bat. The results may not produce a hit—or even contact—but it *should*. In the final analysis, the hitter MUST make the pitcher throw strikes and he must remain focused to produce a well-timed swing. By so doing, he will increase his chances to reach base safely.

Further defining the "quality at-bat recipe," I look for TEN distinct ingredients. For a team to be successful approximately 75% of the time, these ten items *must* play out on a consistent basis. There are more, but they don't necessarily qualify for this article. One of these would be "taking a strike in the final two innings if the hitter did *not* represent the tying or winning run. In the 2002 World Series, in game 2 with the Giants down by two runs in the top of the ninth, Rich Aurelia swung at the *first* pitch from Troy Percival and flied out to left field. Jeff Kent swung at a 1-0 pitch for the second out. Barry Bonds was the third man up. The very best hitter in baseball! Yet, the two guys before him didn't even give him an opportunity to tie or win the game. Bonds hit a home run, but it did no good. The Giants lost 11-10. Watching the game, all I could do was shake my head....

I sort hitters into three hitting "types:" singles/contact, line-drive/gap and pure power. ALL hitters basically fall into one of these categories. Furthermore, to execute a "quality at-bat" ALL hitters must know WHO they are. As my mentor, Ted Williams, used to say, "Hitter know thyself." Singles/contact hitters are not considered "threats" and will be challenged with fastballs in hitters' counts. Therefore, they will walk less. The other hitting types present "threats," and must be pitched to more carefully. The pure power hitter will get off-speed pitches in fastball counts. Often, we see singles/contact hitters with high batting averages, because they can count on fast balls the majority of the time. Pitchers don't feel that these hitters can "hurt" them. It's all a function of the perceived threat. So, the best advice I can give hitters is "know WHO you are!" It will go a long way in establishing your worth to your team and your ultimate grading on the following list.

❏ *#1. Get a good pitch to hit.*

I would suppose that my personal criteria do not deviate too far from what other hitting instructors and coaches would count as their own. Perhaps this article can provide a *checklist* for those who use the term "quality at-bat," but have never really understood its true meaning. Hall of Famer Rogers Hornsby said it as well as anyone in F.C. Lane's book, "Hitting," in the 1920s. "The secret of good batting, in my opinion, is to hit only good balls. Don't be led by impatience to go after bad balls. That's exactly what the pitcher is trying to make you do. That batter should never do what the pitcher wants him to do. When a pitcher gives you a ball to your liking, then is the time to hit it and hit it hard." (The cue "get a good pitch to hit"—normally attributed to Ted Williams—was in fact "borrowed" from Hornsby when Williams was in AAA Minneapolis, prior to Williams getting to the big leagues.)

We're always advising hitters to do this, but *what really is a good pitch to hit?* I have covered this in a previous article and in my videos, but it is worth mentioning again. This cue is probably used more than any other. Whenever I ask a player what HIS definition of a good pitch to hit is, the answer invariably comes back in much the same way Hornsby recited it: "a pitch I can drive." But, in reality, it is much *more* than that. A "good pitch" to hit should be a pitch you have not only *anticipated*, but one that comes in an area that you can handle, with regard to the *count*, the *score*, the *inning*, which *base*(s) is occupied, and your *comfort level* against the pitcher. Okay, let's break some of this down.

Let's say you're right handed, the on-deck hitter in the fifth inning, and your team is down by a run. Your on-deck strategy is to think about how the pitcher has tried to get you out in your previous at bat(s). You've decided he wants to get ahead of you with inside fastballs, and then to put you away with off-speed pitches. So, you're going to look for fastballs early in the count. The lead-off hitter gets a base hit and is on first base. You get the bunt sign from your coach, so your thinking must now change. You're task now is to look for a ball down in the zone, to keep the bunt on the ground, and to advance the runner.

The first pitch is called a high strike, but you feel good knowing that you took it, because it would've been a tough pitch to bunt on the ground. The pitcher then balks the runner to second. The game situation has now changed *again* for you. You look for the sign—and aha!—the bunt is taken off. You've got to re-group. Your first thought now is to get to get the ball on the ground to the right side. Hit behind the runner to get him to third and possibly pick up an RBI if it goes through. You're now looking for a ball out and over the plate. *Up until two strikes*, you're going to take any pitch that's not middle-half away. Here comes the pitch, a slider, down and away. You hit it to the right side, on the ground, but foul. The count goes to 2-1, and you're still looking for that pitch away.

Here it comes, a fastball in the dirt. It gets away from the catcher and the runner winds up on third. You're thinking changes once *again*. Now, you're looking for a ball up in the zone, one you can put in the air to score the runner from third. The 3-1 pitch is a fastball up in your zone. You swing and hit a fly ball that scores the tying run. You executed your plan correctly. You got your "good pitch to hit." But, notice how many times its definition changed during the course of this ONE at bat.

Good hitters are good because they realize that their role can change from pitch to pitch. They make the right mental adjustments. So, when we tell our players to "get a good pitch to hit," we've hopefully gone over this with them beforehand so they understand how quickly the definition of this hitting dynamic can change. This really boils down to having the right *mental approach* at the plate.

❏ *#2. Execute the fundamentals.*

We also talk incessantly about hitting "fundamentals." What is a hitting fundamental? A hitting fundamental is moving a runner from second to third with *nobody* out, or a *hit-and-run* ground ball or hitting the ball on the ground up the middle with a drawn-in infield. Too many times, we *expect* a hitter to execute these fundamentals. But should we? If we want hitters to execute correctly, we must incorporate it into our hitting philosophy. And practice it. DAILY. It must become a part of the coach's routine.

❏ *#3. A sacrifice fly.*

Getting the ball in the air *far enough* with a man on third base is a product of having good mechanics and a good mental plan. The hitter should look for a pitch "up" in the zone until he gets two strikes or alter his *technique* to better "lift" the low pitch.

Recently, I attended a college game in southern California. It was a tie game going into the bottom of the ninth inning. The lead-off man lined a triple to the gap. Man on third, nobody out. The third base coach (the head coach) kept urging his batters to "Get the ball in the air! Get this run in! C'mon! Just a fly ball here." The opposing coach brought in a sinkerball reliever to try to get the hitters to keep the ball on the ground. He did his job well; no pitch was higher than slightly above the knees. Every hitter hit a routine ground ball. Inning over. Runner stranded. The opposing team scored in the top of the tenth and went on to win. The coach of the losing team was furious with his hitters.

JUST a fly ball? When we teach mechanics that make it difficult to get the ball in the air, who are we to blame? Our hitters? Our job as coaches is to put players into positions to succeed, not fail. But, when we march hitters up to the plate with only "one" swing—or a poor hitting philosophy—that is exactly what we are inadvertently doing. We wouldn't send our pitchers to the mound with only one pitch, yet we *routinely* send hitters to the plate with only one swing. And, lament our lack of offense—or blame our hitters.

❏ *#4. Any at-bat that lasts more than eight pitches.*

No one believes in—or tutors—getting "deep in the count" more than I do. This philosophy was deeply ingrained in me by Williams when he managed the Washington Senators.

Today, with the ultra-small strike zones that hitters must cover, taking close pitches becomes routine. In Ted's day (and mine), the strike zone was the armpits to the bottom of the knees. Today, it is the belly-button to the knees. A huge difference. So today, getting deep in the count indeed makes a lot of sense. The more a hitter can see a pitcher (and his *repertoire*), the more success he *should* have. In addition, the idea is to get the pitcher out there to have thrown 100 pitches by the fourth or fifth inning. The goal is to get to the long relievers as quickly as possible. But, wait a minute! EVERY hitter is incapable of executing this task. As a hitting instructor, would you teach Vladimir Guerrero plate discipline? In other words, it's NOT for every hitter, and we must remember that! Not EVERYONE is capable of executing this task.

And, what happens when a hitter faces a "tough" pitcher? Tough pitchers can be defined in two ways. First, the pitcher who is just a top drawer pitcher, able to consistently throw strikes to all four corners of the strike zone and is also able to throw "against the count." By this I mean when the hitter is ahead 1-0, 2-0, 2-1, 3-0, 3-1, the pitcher is able to keep the hitter off guard by throwing off-speed pitches in fast-ball counts. Second, any pitcher who is just "on" that day and making consistently good pitches. When you run up against pitchers like these, you've got to make some concessions and adjustments!

When this happens, the hitter must realize that looking for that "perfect" pitch may be pretty elusive. He's "on" and throwing tough pitches right and left—not "giving in" to the hitter in "predictable" situations. I tell hitters NOT to look for the perfect pitch, but to open up their strike zones and put the ball in play. Too many times, I see hitters taking strikes early in the count, thereby allowing the pitcher to get two strikes on him. When a pitcher is "on" his game like that, he usually winds up putting the hitter away. I know when I played, those good pitchers were "good" because they consistently made good pitches. Getting behind in the count against Nolan Ryan by trying to get deep in the count was practically suicidal. If he got two strikes on you, look out! You've got to give in a little. You've got to adjust. Why make that tough pitcher, tougher?

Now, against pitchers who are not on their game that day—who are not making those tough pitches, you can take some more liberties and look for your pitch, because you know that he doesn't have the stuff that day to "put you away." You can be more selective! And, you must take advantage of this situation.

When I was playing, I had a teammate who absolutely could not hit Nolan Ryan. When Ryan threw his glove out on the mound, he was certain to go 0-4, with three called punch-outs. He talked to anyone and everyone about how he could gain more time. The more people he talked to, the more confused he became (sound familiar?). Nothing seemed to work. Frustration set in. He tried shortening up, bunting for a base hit, moving back in the box, everything. You name it, he tried it. Then, one afternoon at the hotel in Anaheim, before facing Ryan, I talked to him about "hitting zones" and their demotion (or promotion) to accommodate certain-type pitchers. Basically, it was "don't let him get ahead of you by taking pitches. If it's around the plate, put it in play, but don't let him get to two strikes on you." Point to remember: good pitchers are just that—good. When they get two strikes on you, they have the ability to put good hitters away. Anyway, for some reason, it clicked. This made sense to him. He went 2-2 off Ryan that night, with two walks and two line-drive doubles. He changed absolutely nothing mechanically; he just took advantage of some good information.

The majority of hitters hate to hit with two strikes. To be an effective hitter with two strikes, the hitter must adjust to that particular count situation. Effective two-strike hitting implies the confidence that comes from knowing your capabilities and being able to adjust intelligently. Getting deep isn't for *everyone*. A hitter—and his coach— must know his capabilities. Again, putting a player into a situation with no escape can ruin a hitter and his confidence.

❑ *#5. A line-drive out.*

Hitters hit line drives because they are executing their mechanics correctly. To hit a line drive, a hitter has probably "matched the plane of the swing to the plane of the pitch." In Robert Adair's book, *The Physics of Baseball*, he says that the LEVEL swing that produces line drives has a 10° upslope. This type of swing normally produces the line drives that carry to the gaps. When I played, we called these line drives, "ass-and-elbows" line drives. (All you'd see was the outfielder's ass and elbows!) As opposed to the low-line drives that one-hop the infield dirt and produce singles.

In other words, there are two types of line drives—high-line drives and low-line drives. One of my hitting "types" is the *line-drive/gap hitter*. The goal of the line-drive gap hitter is to "balance out" the trajectories of balls off his bat. He normally has "average"-to-"good" foot speed and should hit for high total bases. He may have some power. He should shoot for 50% line drives, 25% fly balls, and 25% ground balls. His position on the axis is slightly behind center, facilitating a slightly steeper swing plane than the singles/contact hitter.

Two distinct examples of this identical hitting type would be Larry Walker and Darren Erstad. Both would be classified as line-drive/gap hitters. Walker has "plus" power and hits 35+ home runs per year, while Erstad hits a ton of singles and doubles. Both are the same type hitter, Walker having a bit more power. As a result, he sits behind the axis somewhat more than Erstad, so each gets different results. Erstad is a low-line drive hitter, and Walker is a high-line drive hitter. However, both are terrific hitters! Line drives are a good indication of efficient and correct mechanics and a good mental hitting approach.

❑ *#6. A walk.*

A walk is acceptable IF the hitter was aggressive when he was ahead in the count. Too many times, I see hitters who eventually walk who had "hit-me" fastballs thrown to them that they took. To them, a "walk is as good as a hit." But, is it?

Again, I am a firm believer in "getting a good pitch to hit." Often, this requires great patience and the ability to hit with two strikes. *Pure power* types *should* be more selective than the lesser threats in the lineup, who will be challenged more. However, there is a very fine line drawn between being "controlled aggressive" and too patient. Hitters must be made aware that "they can expect certain pitches in certain situations," and that "thinking along with the pitcher" makes sense. When he does that, he WON"T be taking those hittable fastballs when he's ahead in the count.

One revealing statistic involves "walks" and "slugging percentage." To the best of my recollection, the 2001 San Diego Padres led the NL in walks, yet were last in slugging percentage. This doesn't make sense! A team with little or no power will be "challenged" by opposing pitchers, because their hitters don't pose multi-base threats. Padre hitters continually got 1-0, 2-0, 3-0, 2-1, 3-1 fast balls for this reason. Yet, their hitters seemed more pre-occupied with taking pitches, than with swinging the bats. Quizzing San Diego's manager, Bruce Bochy, revealed that their offensive plan revolved around "on-base percentage" and "getting deep in the count." Their primary goal was getting to the long relievers early in the game. I have no problem with that, but on-base percentage *in the absence of high slugging percentage* does NOT produce the highly sought-after "OPS" benchmark (the "litmus test" criterion for offensive proficiency). OPS is arrived at by adding On-base Percentage together with Slugging percentage. In other words, the player's overall ability to "get on," plus his ability to "drive in" his teammates.

❑ *#7. A hit-by-pitch.*

Some players seem to make their "living" by getting hit. Those that crowd the plate or "dive" into pitches are more susceptible to this. Additionally, those hitters who have poor mechanics and can't get the hands through in time will also be pitched to inside, and therefore may be hit more often than others.

When I played, if I was hitting against someone I "owned," (a relatively small number), I would do anything I possibly could to AVOID being hit. Conversely, against certain pitchers whom I didn't have much luck against, I would turn *into* the pitch (anything to get on base!). My recollection is that I led the AL in HBPs in 1972.

❑ *#8. A hit.*

This is a no-brainer. ANY hit—*duck snort, Texas leaguer, Baltimore chop, broken bat, flare, dinker.* No matter; they ALL count!

❑ *#9. Working the count.*

Once again, if executed in a timely and correct way, working the count is a thing of beauty, especially with the shrinking strike zones we see in major league baseball.

Unfortunately, at the lower amateur levels, umpiring is markedly erratic, thereby making "working the count" pretty tough. The best rule of thumb is "don't help a wild pitcher." If he's not throwing consistent strikes, you MUST work the count.

Many coaches say that quality at-bats are not about hits. Many coaches believe that quality at bats are obtained by fighting a pitcher off, by fouling balls and working hard to keep the at-bat "alive." I can understand the rationale behind this thought process, but personally, my *experience* makes me somewhat cynical. I believe the operative word missing from this thought-process is "tough," as in "tough pitches."

Often, we hear announcers saying, "What a great at-bat! Smith has really worked the count well by fouling off pitches." However, what I saw was two of the pitches Smith fouled off were fastballs (while ahead in count) right down the middle; he was *late* on both of them. My thought was that Smith probably should be standing on second base—instead of being congratulated for ultimately making an out, because he "made the pitcher pitch." Just my two cents.

❏ *#10. Using the middle of the field with a drawn-in infield.*

The best place to hit the ball with a drawn-in infield is a ground ball right back through the middle of the diamond. The percentages favor the hitter doing this. What we normally see, however, is players trying to hit a sacrifice fly. This can also be an "okay" approach, but the hitter's plan when he goes to the plate should be relative to the pitcher and what his best pitch is. In other words, if his best pitch is high cheese, he should try to stay on top of the pitch by leveling off his shoulders. If he's facing a sinkerballer, he's got to try to hit it hard on the ground. He will not have much success trying to hit a high fast ball on the ground—and *vice versa*.

The "Key" Consideration

One important point to remember is to always make a sincere attempt to field a well-balanced lineup. This factor was reflected by what we saw in the 2002 World Series, when home runs produced late-inning wins. Always keep in mind that a place exists for all hitting types and approaches. Just make sure the players being asked to do them are well-suited for the task-at-hand.

ABOUT THE AUTHOR

Mike Epstein is one of America's top hitting analysts and favorite instructors, having spoken at the American Baseball Coaches Association and other high profile conventions. Prior to Mike's teaching years, he was an all-American baseball player and still holds the highest lifetime batting average of .384 at the University of California, Berkeley. He was a member of the first United States Olympic baseball team, leading the team in many offensive hitting categories in Japan (1964). He was named the Sporting News and Topps Minor League Player-of-the-Year in 1966.

Mike played for the Baltimore Orioles, Washington Senators, Oakland A's, Texas Rangers, and California Angels from 1966 through 1974. He broke a longstanding Senators' record for lefties by hitting 30 home runs in 1969, culminating in winning the American League Player Win Average Award, given to the league's most productive offensive player (Willie McCovey won it in the National League). Mike also became one of a very select few in Major League history by belting four home runs in four consecutive at bats in 1971. He also led the World Champion Oakland A's in home runs in 1972.

Mike Epstein continued his career in baseball as a minor league manager and hitting coordinator, which has led to his current career as one of baseball's leading independent hitting instructors and consultants for baseball and softball. For more information, go to www.mikeepsteinhitting.com